BROOKER's
VILLAGE-ON-SEA
Stories from Post-World War II

CHARLOTTE KENDRICK

700 – 838 West Hastings St. Vancouver, BC V6C 0A6
www.explorabooks.com
Phone: (604) 330 67951

Published by Explora Books 2024

ISBN: 978-1-998394-00-5

FOREWORD

After the unconditional surrender of Germany on 8 May, 1945, the citizens of England had to adjust their previous years of home war effort routines into ordinary daily life.

The echoes of continued fighting in Japan, hung over them and they couldn't quite give up their Home Guard, Civil Defense and other auxiliaries that were organized into communities to serve their country at home.

Rationing would slowly give way for needed purchases, but for now they were still looking forward to the day for food, clothing, and utilities to become available.

Included in these expectations were fears as they continued to watch for the enemy planes that might continue to fly over their country and drop bombs in diverse places. An uneasy feeling that without notice the enemy might return and continue their efforts to take over their beloved county and that the surrender of Germany was just a ploy for Japan to start sending their Zero's to take the place of the German Messerschmitt.

This story starts in the middle part of May, several days after the war ended and just before the surrender of Japan, which would not be until August 15, 1945.

Even though this book takes a lighter side of their plight of returning to normality, it does not for a moment take away their outstanding valor.

This book is dedicated to the British and what they taught us from their wonderful examples of 'how to cope', 'make do', 'mend' and to accept their lot in life under such horrendous conditions.

I hope if the United States ever comes under attack and especially for the length of time Britain was at war that we would be able to endure and bring out the brave and courageous traits they did.

I love the British and I thank them for their sterling examples of… endurance and loyalty. They have made me proud to know my family roots are there.

Winston Churchill pleaded with them "Never give up. Never give up. Never give up", which became their motto and they never, never, never gave up.

CHAPTER ONE

The deep purple night drew its curtain over the golden remains of the day and disappeared with the soft melodic sound of the waves that washed upon the shores of the small southern coastal village overlooking the English Channel.

Yet, this mesmerizing picture was not enough to ease Anise Brooker's ingrained war mind-set that continued to haunt her and found herself ill at ease with the feeling that this was only the quiet before the storm.

Her heart yearned to brush away the lingering sensation that a German Messerschmitt was about to appear and suddenly touch off the terrifying routine to once again run for cover.

Though she knew the war had ended officially earlier that month the built in armor of self-defense still inundated her, as it did with all the inhabitants of Brooker's Village-On-Sea.

The beach projected its perfect splendor that evening as she tried once again to reconcile her uneasy spirit to relax and just enjoy the beauty that surrounded her.

Her calm demeanor had been the reassuring factor in her relationship with her younger sister's more enthusiastic one, creating the inner conflict she was experiencing at that moment and was trying to conquer before returning home.

This was her favorite time of the day and was the time to recount the day's activities and put the events to good use for the future. She liked to recall a lesson she might have been taught. Her parents had instilled that in her and her younger sister, Cinny, to recount the events at the end of the day and see what they were taught and what they could have done better to meet the challenges, however small or large they might have experienced.

Even though Mr. and Mrs. William Brooker, had been killed in a London Blitz in the early part of the war their words would continue to be instilled in her.

Her tired body though strong and healthy weighted down from the years of war began to let her understand the burdens that had been placed upon her. The way she carried herself was still graceful and drew attention from the customers she served each day and would comment how lovely she was and the big question why wasn't she ever married?

There had not been an easy answer to their questions all she knew was that she had to take care of business and her younger sister making sure their lives and the family business would be secure.

The sisters worked side by side completely in unison. The contrast of personalities had not affected their relationship but only enhanced it. Anise was the serious minded one with a soft demeanor and voice. With the responsibility of being the older sister she felt at times older than the five years apart.

Anise Brooker walked leisurely with her usual graceful movement.

Her light brown hair streaked by the sun added blonde that framed her soft peaches and cream face.

With large hazel eyes she was very attractive but had never been interested in any of the young men in the village. She had been so involved with surviving no one had ever caught her attention.

Her imagination and self-confidence completed the attractive person turning thirty.

Her younger sister Cinny was more outgoing and carefree her bright red hair and sparkling blue eyes magnified her beautiful expressive face.

With the new feeling life was changing made her comprehend she had not been as careful about her appearance as she could have been.

She slowly climbed the old graying steps from the beach up to the family cottage that had been built by her great grandfather, John Brooker, in the early 1800's.

Her mood was lifted as she became aware of the familiar glowing fire she could see through the large bay window that faced the channel and magnified the warm feeling she was able to glean through her self-talk from the peaceful walk on the beach.

The freedom of not having the black curtains that once draped the windows was daunting. To be able to peer through clear paned windows at night made her feel uneasy for at that moment she wanted to run inside and put them up again, so she took a deep breath of acceptance that the war was truly over as she went through the well-worn wooden door.

"Cinny, are you home?" Anise called as she hung her sweater on the wooden coat rack in the warm entryway and smiled at her sister sitting on the faded green braided rug in front of the fireplace resting her back on the aged green wing backed chair. She settled down beside her finding peace and comfort from her younger sister.

"Yes, I'm just reading, trying to get sleepy so I can go to bed and sleep and not toss and turn all night like I usually do. I am tired, but I can't turn off the thoughts that keep popping up."

"I was thinking the same thing; maybe as time goes by we will be able to relax and get more accustomed to not having a war going on and the fear to run for cover. I have just been trying to convince myself that the war is truly over and we have no worries. I just know with the length of time we've been under such terrifying circumstances for these past six years, will take some time for us all to train ourselves into new routines void of self-preservation. Don't you agree?"

"I suppose so; you always have a way of coming through with comforting words. Wish I had more of your maturity… I… I didn't mean you're old…I meant…"

"Relax, my little Cinnamon, I know what you mean, five years difference in our ages is quite a bit. It gave me more memories with Mum and Dad though than you. I am grateful I can remember things they taught, or tried to teach us, they were excellent parents. We must try to carry on so they will be proud of us…. As a matter of fact we did make it through the war and we should celebrate.

"Hold on don't get carried away."

"I know, it is just really sinking in just a habit I guess. I do want us to have some sort of closure though, let's see what the rest of the village is thinking; we can all pool our resources and make a 'Brooker's Village-On-Sea" celebration for the 'end of the war. Will you help me?"

"Of course, but don't come up with any wild ideas you might have in mind!"

"Whatever do you mean?"

"Well, for example." The younger sister said setting her book down.

"There was the time you wanted us all to dress up as our favorite animal for the Halloween party one year, and you made me the back
end of your horse costume from school.

Now, don't say a word until I have completely finished. Remember when you insisted I wear that silly pink crepe paper flower costume, remember how incredibly silly I looked? That gritty crunched up petal flower dress and make shift hat that matched and kept falling over the one side of my face, and made me feel I was tipsy and couldn't control myself?"

Anise started to laugh at Cinny's review of the past episodes of costumes and couldn't catch her breath. She doubled over from the out of control laughter as the images became brighter and brighter then spread to Cinny when they both started to laugh remembering the silly things they had been through together.

"Remember when mummy put her hat on dad while he was sleeping in this chair, his favorite green winged back chair?

When he woke up and one of the feathers was poking him in the ear and he jumped up and started running around the room hitting himself on the head over and over?

I thought we would never stop laughing at him. He really got mad at us which made it even funnier."

"…and the time he slid down the banister showing us how he used to have fun as a boy and caught a splinter in his…ahem…bottom?"

"I'd forgotten all about that and mummy had to shut him up in the bathroom, and take it out while you and I stood outside laughing so hard while he was yelling at her,' careful, now careful…ouch, ouch, ouch, ouch, damn, damn, DAMN, that hurts."

"Oh yes and remember when the cat got stuck in the tree and he had to call the fire department to bring a long ladder?

When they finally got here, Dad was stuck there too? Mum had to ask the Fire Brigade to get both the cat and Dad down?"

"Ooooo, I'd forgotten that, he was so mad at that cat he almost gave it away and we had to stop him?"

By this time both sisters were rolling on the large green rug in front of the fireplace wiping tears from their faces.

After calming down from their laughter from the simple things they had experienced with their parents and each other.

Stoking the fire and clearing her throat Anise said softly and sat back down hugging her knees. "I wish we could be with them now that we are older and let them know how much we love them and to be able to tell them what wonderful memories we have of our childhood, but maybe they know, maybe they can see us where ever Heaven is…"

"I agree, I know they are in Heaven, if they don't make it there, I know we sure won't!" Cinny exclaimed

"I hope someday you and I will have children and they will have some good memories of us the way we do with Mum and Dad."

"Well, Annie, in order to do that we need to provide them with a father. Do you suppose we will get married someday? Since the war is over, maybe there will be a chance…" Cinny's voice trailed off into thoughts of her future.

"I don't know little one, for me anyway, maybe, it's because I am feeling old. I am turning 30 next month. I don't think I will, but we never know for sure. Miracles do happen!" She laughed looking into Cinny's shinning blue eyes. "I am sure you will though." Her words trailed off into dreamy contemplation. Shaking off the thoughts of marriage Anise jumped up and said

"Let's have some cocoa before we go to bed? Cinny asked getting up off the floor"…and maybe a biscuit or two?" She added.

"Yes, little Cinnamon, a "bekee" or two."

"Anise, do you like your name? I've always wished they hadn't named us after spices, don't you?"

"Well, little sister, I used to wonder about that too. It could have been that you had Cinnamon color hair. I don't know why my name was Anise. I am just grateful they were bakers and not farmers. Think about it this way, they could have named us after animals instead of naming us after spices … we could have been named …'Bunny' and 'Piggy'".

Anise took a deep breath sitting back down on the floor after she tried to reconcile her sister.

Then she started to laugh again thinking about what their names could have been, which sparked another round of laughter and they lay on the floor again, bringing both sister to laughter again as Cinny chocked out, "Yes, I never thought about it that way before, thank goodness they were bakers and not farmers."

"You know, laughing makes me feel so good. Let's promise each other that from now on we will ask each other before we go to bed if we've had a good laugh today, OK?" Anise asked catching her breath once more.

"Yes, lets, I was thinking the same thing, I feel so much better about everything, but we must not just say this tonight, but actually do it.

I think the whole village needs to laugh and relax. We need to be grateful we did make it through the war together, we kept our businesses going in spite of everything, fear, rationing and losing family members these past six years."

"Maybe we can put these humorous efforts into a village celebration."

"Of course, that is a great idea. It could help us all to focus on the positive things we have endured. Let's start talking to everyone tomorrow."

The two siblings sat close together gazing into the fireplace as they each contemplated the future sipping their hot chocolate and slowly nibbling on their biscuits they had made in their bakery that day.

CHAPTER TWO

Brooker's village was built on top of a hill overlooking the English Channel where the Brooker's family cottage, teashop and bakery, was located and overlooked rows of white faced shops with brown tiled roofs that faced each other with the church at the bottom of the hill that continued down to a valley of dark green hedged verdant fields of local farmers.

The church and vicarage was built before Captain Brooker founded the village. He decided by building shops to entice his longtime friends and family might inhabit the beautiful area, and now looking upwards the fruits of his and his friend's labor at the well cared for small adjacent businesses.

The glint of sun announced another new day as it pierced through the immaculately clean white kitchen, which served both the Brooker's teashop and bakery. The beginning of a sunny day helped brighten both sisters' moods as they prepared for the days needed baked goods for their customers and organize the day's work with the youth that worked for them in various positions from cooks, bakers, waitresses, to the cleanup crew.

"Polly, please be more careful when you pour the tea, Mrs. Odette made a complaint yesterday about the way she was served as it splattered onto her new suit. Sorry, I know we have been busier than usual, but we will get more servers as soon as possible when we see who is staying on here and not returning home."

"I am sorry but there were customers so impatient with me wanting more tea I didn't realize I dropped some on her, we do need more help if it is going to be this congested. We also need more help keeping everything filled. I tried to get a pot of tea for the vicar's wife and there was none."

"I know, we are working on that now. Thank you for all your hard work, and we will pay more as soon as we can, so just be patient with us and we will be patient with you as well."

"Cinny, will you help me set the tables in the tea shop? I want to use the new table cloths we made?"

"Sure, just a minute I need to get the buns out of the oven that are almost done and will be there to help."

Anise carried the neatly folded burgundy linen cloths and napkins to the tea shop area and sat them down on the counter feeling very satisfied how much they would add to the old wooden tables and chairs her parents had purchased years before. Well-worn but with the sister's routine polishing with loving care were still suitable for the village customers.

They had received help from the youth that had been relocated there during the war and now some were considering staying there and not to return to their families in London and maybe stay in the small cottages the neighbors had built for their comfort since they were so far from home and family. Several of them had lost their families in bombings and some just wanted to stay on with the friendships they had formed, and some would eventually marry their sweethearts they had met in the small village.

The war did indeed furnish many blessings as well as painful losses and the key they found in Brooker's Village-On-Sea, was their relationships. Even the acquaintances that were not always understood, but that had not mattered, as their motto had been all for one and one for all….yes, they did indeed feel a deep kinship of some degree with each and every one they had met.

"Annie, I love the table cloths! The color will be good to hide most stains, you think of everything."

"You give me way too much credit…but this fabric was on a great sale and I couldn't resist it, but yes it just so happened to be good to not show stains. We need to take a trip to London soon and visit Uncle Reggie; I wanted to see if he would paint Mum and Dad's portrait to put on the wall facing the fireplace. You remember the picture of them on their wedding day. The one where Mum was in her beautiful white wedding gown and Dad was in his black tux? Wouldn't that be nice to have that enlarged as a painting to remember them by, even when we are gone?"

"That would be ever so nice. I would like to see all the family in London, well, the ones that are left. I mean…"

"I know what you are trying to say, the ones not killed when Mum and Dad were. It would be good for us to see London and how it looks now. I am sure it will be different. It may be a hard time for us, but we need to visit Uncle Reggie and Aunt Lily, I am so thankful they are alive and well.

Let's ask Mr. Grainger if he will check out the "M G" and see if she will get us to London. I want to drive with the top down and enjoy the countryside and stop in some of the places on the way when they would drive us on the A-22 to London. How does that sound, Cinny?"

"Oh, all right and we could have a shopping day as well, we have not spent money in so long wouldn't it be great fun to shop, and eat good food in London? That is if we can find places that can serve good food."

"That would be nice to take a little trip to relax and see family. I need some new shoes too, for work and for church." Anise added.

"Let's get our hair done up and buy some make up too, I heard on the radio about some new cosmetics from advertisements. I'd like to look like Veronica Lake and wear my hair over one eye and look mysterious." The younger sister said as she pulled a red curl over one of her large blue eyes.

"Now, Cinny, I'm not sure you and I could ever be the mysterious type, aren't we too countrified? We are more like Anne of Green Gables." Anise said trying not to laugh at her younger sister's sudden attempt at being glamorous and remembered her own thoughts about taking better care of herself.

"I suppose you're right, but I still want to see what new things the
London shops have, you won't spoil my fun with that now will you Annie?"

"No, I won't spoil your fun, I want to enjoy our trip so you do whatever you want, and as long it is not too outlandish."

"Oh all right, take the fun out of it I'll keep it as normal as I can." She promised at the exhilarating feeling of seeing London once again.

The teashop started to fill with customers for the day and the young owners scurried about making sure they were served properly and that the tea and food was up to the high standards their parents had instilled in them.

CHAPTER THREE

The time worn gray stone vicarage was quiet except for the chatter of Hazel Grovenor, the vicar's wife.

The golden morning sun brought warmth through the paned windows and highlighted the antique furniture. The dull brown tweed fabric of the chairs and sofas revealed the consumption of past tears and laughter.

Hazel had added brass lamps and large plants throughout the house which brought out the richness of the thick mahogany library paneled walls.

Hazel herself was kind and caring about everyone in the village even though she did have a reputation of knowing everyone's life.

Her tall stature added to her commanding yet composed personality. With graying blonde hair she still had the touch of beauty that her husband admired.

Richard Grovenor was tall with dark hair turning gray at the temples, giving him the distinguished look; the way a vicar should look. His soft gray eyes could penetrate his parishioners allowing them the confidence they would need to be able to discuss their problems safely with him. His quiet reserve contrasted with his more outgoing wife and did not want to stifle her creative energies so he allowed her room to live her life free of his intrusion.

Their marriage could at times be confrontational but with maturity they had allowed each other to communicate personal even though opposite views and come to a peaceful understanding.

The couple did complement each other and served the community well which in the end had become their family as they had no children of their own and most of their family either passed away or lived such a distance they had lost contact.

"Hazel, please, let me finish my sermon for Sunday. I am having a hard enough time trying to put my thoughts down on paper without you interrupting me every five minutes. Please, now what do you want?" He asked scratching his head.

"Richard, I am trying to tell you about what I heard … well about Les Corbett. He was drunk again and was staggering down the street singing rude songs from the first war. Can't you do anything with him? Talk to him or do something? He and Nigel are an embarrassment to our whole village."

"Now, now, Hazel, we must not judge too harshly, they were injured you know in the first war and never married. I have tried to talk to them about their drinking but we never get very far as they start crying about how terrible the war was. Then they each tell me some of their worn out stories about war experiences. I think they have magnified after telling the same ones over and over and exaggerating them but I listen any way. They must need attention, heaven knows they are all alone, well except for each other and of course they are not helpful with overcoming their problem but help steep themselves in self-pity during their drinking nights."

"They were not injured that badly as you know, well physical injuries and probably are more emotional scars.

Remember that nice little widow woman, Mrs. Bradley? She liked Les I could tell. I think she could not stand his drinking though.

He does have family around, but he is so drunk most of the time when he is out of his tailor's shop his drunken state chases everyone away, with the exception of Nigel as you said are birds of a feather, but at least Les is clean and dapper where poor Nigel needs…well he needs to smarten himself up and get some clean clothes."

"Hazel, once more, let them alone. If you want to try to do any reformation, you have my blessing. Just remember, be careful not to offend, they at least come to service. Don't make things worse for them."

"Well, I might try to help. They just need a good woman's advice from time to time."

"Yes dear, give them some good woman's advice." The vicar's thoughts went back to his unfinished sermon.

"I want to help them stop drinking before they are in a horrendous accident or hurt someone else. It can only be a matter of time before something dreadful happens because of not being in control of themselves and their surroundings."

"I agree, I have thought that as well, we only have so many chances in this life and if we make bad choices too many times we will run out of luck. So please do your best, just keep in mind it will take some time and you won't be able to see miracles overnight. I didn't want to get involved but suppose that is my job, to be involved with my parishioners"

"Yes, it is your job Richard that is true, and I know it could be very dodgy to get involved. It will take some time and I must be patient. Do you suppose I should ask someone to help me in this endeavor?"

"I shouldn't think so, if you do include someone else there will surely be gossip about it, and might turn it into something untoward. Be silent in your well doing my love. We can't afford to encourage talk about this for it would surely get back to them and there would be additions from gossip. No, keep it to yourself and be very discrete about it."

"Of course you are right, and I will act the same way any of you men act when caught doing something odd…pretend not to acknowledge and don't have any idea of what they are talking about. You chaps do that quite well." She laughed as she saw the puzzled look on her husband's face and kissed him on the forehead goodbye.

CHAPTER FOUR

The village's small grocery store lined with sturdy wooden shelves filled with carefully organized canned and packaged goods in their proper order had been opened early as usual by its proprietor Ronald Simon.

The aroma of fresh ground coffee for his morning customers filled the well-organized limited space.

He prepared the shelves to be stocked with as many items as it had been allotted. The early peace time was reflecting some of the loosening grip of store items and lessened the need of black market items they all tried to reach without guilt.

The fresh produce stand needed to be placed outside as soon as he carefully arranged the variety of fruit and vegetables in their usual pattern he devised to bring out the bright colors that completed each other.

The tinkling bell announced the arrival of a customer.

He ran his fingers through his thick dark hair and prepared to wait on the well-groomed woman that gracefully came through the door of the small carefully cleaned grocery store.

As usual Ron gave the attractive woman the once over as he did with all the pretty females that came through the door.

"May I help you he smiled?" His nice smile, tall stature, dark hair and blue eyes were always a beacon for women.

"Yes, I need some meat for dinner tonight. What do you have that is fresh? "She asked smiling demurely up at him.

"Ronald, I will help the lady, you need to tend to the back room and finish the produce table." His wife, Olive said, who was also tall and very attractive with her dark hair and large expressive brown eyes, interrupted his conversation with the attractive customer.

This was an everyday occurrence for them, as her husband was very fond of the ladies. Olive had gotten very polished at running interception between her husband and a nice-looking female no matter what age she might be.

"We have some beef that would make a nice meal. How much do you want?"

"Is this a beef roast?" The dark haired woman asked with a knowing smile of what this interfering wife had so smoothly accomplished.

"Yes, it is and very fresh. We have a nice five pound one, or a smaller three pound, would that be what you need?"

"The three pound would do nicely here's my ration book. Thank you."

"Thank you, come again." Olive said handing the pre-wrapped roast and ration book back to the surprised customer as she paid for the purchase and closed the door behind her gently.

"Ron, are you e v e r going to stop this horrible habit of chatting up every woman that comes into the store?" She turned as she asked her husband coming back into the front of the store.

"I don't pay attention to e v e r y woman that comes through the door."

"That's true; you only make advances to the attractive ones."

"What's wrong with smiling at customers and making them comfortable in the store?"

"Nothing, but just you be careful, you try my patience and one day you will toy with the wrong one and she will take you up on your advances…then what would you do?"

"What do you mean take me up on my advances my love?" He kept grinning at her.

"You know full well what I mean… those big grinned advances that you make. You will get into trouble one day, and I'm telling you now, I am tired of you doing this. You forget you are a married man, with a wife who is your partner and that I am always here with you."

"Yes, love I do always remember I have a wife who is always here." He replied still smiling and grabbing his dust cloth to hurry off from the confrontation avoiding her fiery glare each time he put her through this routine.

"Just you remember what I am saying that's all." She said returning to the back room office to finish her inventory she had stopped for the halting of her husband's advances to the attractive customer.

Turning around to finish scolding of her errant husband Olive found he had vanished as he usually did.

Next-door, at the chemist shop was also busy that sunny morning preparing for the day's customers.

The small shop perfectly filled with an assortment of necessities that was cleaned and dusted each day.

Collin Jarvis had recently returned from his service in the army where he had been stationed in France. He was experiencing the same issues other returned veterans had to do to acclimatize back to civilian life.

With a medium build, light brown hair and blue eyes he was constantly under scrutiny from all the young women in the surrounding area as a possible husband.

"Collin, please hurry, we need to open, get those shelves stocked and hurry." Ivy Jarvis, his older sister asked her younger brother trying to get him up to the task of their chemist shop.

"I am Ivy, slow down and let me get back to normal. I am doing my best. You have to be patient with me." He said trying not to show agitation with her constant prodding him with his slow pace, which he was trying to speed up even without her provocation.

Ivy was upset with her father, Ralph, who wanted to retire and leave the shop. Since Collin had returned from the war Ralph had not been too involved in the business and left most of it up to her. It had been her source of refuge since her husband Darryl's death and was grateful to have something to pour herself into which she had been and thoroughly.

One day he thought he would have to talk to his sister and let her know that he did not want the shop and it would be all hers. He had other ideas for his future and it was not his plan to continue to work in the family chemist shop.

Across the street and up on the corner facing the Brooker's Tea Shop and Bakery was the Rutledge Antique Shop. There too was a father ready to retire and leave his store to his son who also would be returning from France.

Henry Rutledge counted the days until Matt would come home, and with joy knew his son had survived the war and was in good health to have a bright future now in peacetime.

To look forward to the day his son would take over his business, marry and make him a grandfather that was what he made plans for since the war ended.

He had already made his family known who lived in and was going to move to Cornwall. Since his wife passed away the year before he could hardly contain his sadness and mourned deeper than he could have ever imagined.

Every item in the shop reminded him of her.

The only escape would be to move and be with his sister and brother that still lived where they grew up.

Next door, Clive Odette, the very dapper president of the Brooker's Village bank unlocked the door to start his day.

His small frame didn't detract from his polished appearance and with light gray hair which added a touch of class.

Each morning he would check with the one watchman he hired that stayed in the back room each night.

After he received the nightly report and walked to his office he became aware of the familiar aroma of the fresh pot of coffee that his secretary would buy each morning from the Brooker's Tea Shop along with the equally as fresh pastries.

He went into his recently redecorated office where he started his day. His wife Missy loved to make changes to the office with new Venetian blinds and kept it not only clean but also painted. Since being made the manager of the bank, he found it had not been an easy job during the trying times of the past several years.

The shiny black phone rang and started his new day sitting at his mammoth mahogany desk he smiled when he heard his wife's soft voice.

"Hello, Missy, yes, I remember, I will stop off after work at the grocers and bring the milk and the dog bones home. Anything else?" He smiled thinking about his twenty five year marriage to the lovely Missy Colton.

He fell in love with her the first time he saw her dancing with his friend at a community dance in Woldford.

Her full long blond hair and slim silhouette enticed him to the point he lost a friend over her when he saw them dancing together when they were all at university in London.

The couple had not been able to have children and had adopted stray animals left to starve during the war years. It had helped them to have something to share tender loving care for in a meaningful way. They too were involved in the community affairs.

"Yes, my love, I will be home half past five."

Placing the phone down gently his thoughts were on the future of the banking world. He had heard about changes and new modern technology that would be coming soon and he hoped he would be able to keep up with the new world that would be opening up concerned he might not be able to keep up with them and apply them into the small village bank. Would he have to be replaced with a younger man that would be trained in such techniques?

Hopefully if possible would be approved he wanted to hire an assistant to help him update the solidly run bank.

The doctor's surgery next door to the bank was quiet for the morning hours. Usually there were one or two patients waiting for him.

George Burkhart wore rumpled suits on his medium frame that took away from a handsome face and tousled light brown hair.

"Dr. Burkhart, Mrs. Wilson needs to talk to you again. Do you have the time?" His receptionist, Margery asked covering the phone not to let the patient hear her question.

"Yes, I do, thank you. Hello, Mrs. Wilson, how are you this fine morning?" He asked knowing there would be a negative answer he would receive from the contentious woman he always dreaded. He of course had to endure it for the sake of her husband that he had such high regard for the man's stamina and endurance living with his wife.

"I am sorry to hear that, you should come in and I will take a look. Maybe it is just a sprain. It might not be a break. How did you hurt your leg? Oh, my word, that might be serious, here's Margery, make an appointment with her, see you later." He said smiling and handing her the phone back curious about the story he would be hearing soon. She was inventive he had to admit that about all her never ending aches and pains.

"Doctor, Lucy is here to see you."

"Yes, yes tell her to come in."

Lucy Burkhart was a small woman with graying brown hair pulled up on her head making her appear taller than she actually was. Her piercing blue eyes were no match for her husband as he would turn into jelly each time he saw her. Their children grown and married lived away from them and now they would be grandparents shortly. They both waited happily for the great event.

"Lucy, is everything all right?"

"Yes, everything is all right, you are now a full-fledged grandfather of a bouncing baby boy. Guess what his name is?"

"I couldn't begin to know what it is, tell me, please, sit down my sweetheart." He smiled sitting down at his paper piled desk.

"Well, they named him George and they want to call him 'Georgie'. Isn't that wonderful?" She said jumping up from the well-worn chair facing him.

"That is nice, but, Georgie, I don't know about that, doesn't' sound odd?"

"Odd? I thought it sounded, nice, now that you mention it… Georgie hmm"

"We have to get packed; will you do that for me? I need to arrange my patients to see Dr. Weston. Let's leave tomorrow. I can't wait to see little George uh Georgie."

"Of course, I'll leave now and do our packing and be ready to go early in the morning, Grandpa." She giggled as she left his office.

The quiet tailor shop next door to the surgery was empty as well.

Les Corbett straightened the shelves in his shop then climbed into the white paned window to refold some of the shirts and smoothed and re hung the silk ties of his tailor's shop's display.

As he climbed out of the window, he rubbed his head waiting for the aspirin to take effect to relieve his usual hangover headache. 'I might have to ease up on the drinking, these headaches are getting worse, maybe tomorrow I'll start slowing down on my drinking. I'm not as young as I used to be.' He thought as he stepped out of the window onto the floor.

After completing his preparations to make the shop appealing for his customers, he brushed his thick graying hair into place, patted the sweet Jasmine aftershave on his pale face hoping to bring color to his cheeks, and noted the puffiness under his steel gray eyes.

He peered into the full-length mirror realizing just how old he was. His aging appearance did not help his lonely feelings that day. He had been reviewing his life and it had turned out to be nothing as he thought it had turned out to be.

When he was young, he loved the thoughts of becoming a husband and eventually a father, but the First World War had come soon after he had finished university and was side tracked and lost all perspective of goals he'd once had.

The grizzly scenes haunted him and large quantities of alcohol could not wash away the horror he had encountered over thirty years ago.

His father had passed away several years ago leaving him totally alone to run his father's business that he inherited and wanted to keep it the successful business it had been since Les Corbett Sr. opened it in 1910.

He could feel the past was catching up with him and had better take better care of his health.

CHAPTER FIVE

The dusty old black farm truck made its way through the 'APPLEGATES FARM' entrance winding slowly around the dark green hedge-lined dirt road up to the farmhouse that had been built by the great grandparents of Phil Gates, who had been friends of Anise and Cinnamon Brooker's great grandfather who from an invitation to live near him, settled there so many years before.

Phil was a hardworking farmer that thoroughly enjoyed the family inheritance.

His clean appearance was an amazing feature considering all the dirt, mud, animal fertilizer and sweat he would go through each work day.

His muscular frame, shinning brown hair and large brown eyes that shinned each time he see his lovely wife kept their marriage alive and vibrant.

He rubbed his ears trying to sooth them from the extra loud noises the chickens were making as he drove them to the poultry house that had just been cleaned and repainted by Robert and Ryan Murphy, the seventeen-year-old twins that had been relocated there a few years earlier.

Robert was the leader of the two and more outgoing than Ryan. He was the brains of the group of young men including his twin.

They were tall and lanky. Rob had lighter hair than Ry and blue eyes where the other brother had light gray.

Both boys had the same innocent good looks that the Gates family found hard to stay mad at them for long when one of their little ideas would fail.

Their parents had sent them there for safety, to protect them from the tragedies happening in London.

Phil brought the old truck to a stop as he jumped out to inspect their work.

"Good job. You boys are such good workers I want you to take a few days off and do something you have wanted to do. Maybe go back home to London and visit some of your family that is still there, maybe your aunt that sends you letters and packages? How does that sound? "He said surveying the excellent job they had done for him and wanted to repay them for their hard work. For not only that particular job but also all the work they had done for him since their arrival two years earlier.

"Well, maybe, we'll think about it and will get back to you with something, is that all right, Mr. Gates?" Ryan asked politely. Even though the boys had been in trouble from time to time with their inventive schemes, they were polite.

"Of course, you and Robert talk it over and let me know what you decide." He said walking into the renovated chicken house.

The two walked down the path to the immense vegetable fields to start watering for the day and continue their usual work routine.

"What do you think Rob, should we take a trip to see Auntie Mary? I don't know if I want to see London, now that mum and dad wont' be there and our house won't be their either. How do you feel about going back?"

"The same, Ry, I don't think I can stand to see the rubble and the remains of our street we used to live on. I've been dreading the day we would have to go back there, have you felt that way too?"

"Yes, the same feelings of dread. We have been living in denial so long I hate to burst our happy little bubble we've existed in these past two years. When we first came mum and dad were alive, then....."

"I know, then the news came they had been killed. I still have a hard time with it. I can't think about them being gone. No, I do not want to go back. We could do something else; we could go to Wellerton and see what they have for supplies so we can finish some our projects."
"While there we could also see a movie, we haven't seen one is so long." Rob said wanting to escape the cruelty of war.

"That sounds good to me. We have to spend the night though, it's at least fifty kilometers and how do we get there?"

"We will ask Mr. Gates, he'll get us there, but I don't know where we will stay though."

"He'll have an idea, I'm sure. He always has an idea."

"What about Homer? He needs to come with us, don't you think?" Ryan asked.

"Yes, he needs to come with us. He worked as hard as we did. We could not have finished so soon if he hadn't lent a hand. He can help us get what we need.

I'll ask tonight at supper."

The aroma of Irene Gates' dinner filled the boys with cheerful memories of their mother several years earlier when they would come home after school tired and hungry. She did remind them of her. They were both soft and gentle, always working hard to clean, cook and be there for the days needs the family would have.

Her lovely expressive face had a natural peach blush with long auburn hair she always brought upon her head neat and tidy. With sparkling green eyes she was Phil's reason he would always sing, "Good Night Irene".

Irene had been one of the reasons the boys had been able to cope with the tragic news of their parent's death. Her warm smile, and love and concern for them had been therapeutic enough to get them through their mourning and draw on her strength to get them through their mourning.

"Hello, boys, wash up and we will eat. Mr. Gates and Homer aren't here but should be at any moment." She said wiping her hands on her bright yellow apron. Irene could be quite attractive when she dressed up for the Sunday Services.

"Sure, but do you need us to do anything for you before we wash?" Rob asked.

"No, but thank you, I may have some things tomorrow though. We can talk about that in the morning at breakfast."

"Sounds good to me, we're starved!" Ryan almost yelled going up the stairs to the bathroom.

"Hi love, how was your day?" Phil asked her with a broad grin looking at her with approval.

"It was a good day, got a lot of things caught up that I had to put off until now. So glad to be on schedule…"

"You and your schedule, I don't know why that is so important to you. It seems you are always working so how can you not be on schedule?" He laughed picking her up and hugging her tightly.

"Oh, you!" She said giggling at his sudden quixotic bear hug.

"Homer! I didn't see you, the twins are upstairs washing up, please, join them." Irene said as her husband gently put her back down on the floor.

"Yes, thank you, I will." He said blushing trying to leave as quickly as possible from the site of them in their embrace.

CHAPTER SIX

The rustle of paper grew louder as Anise laid her well-worn book, Jane Austen's "Pride and Prejudice ", down on her large rose floral feather bed. She slid to the floor and tip toed to the door where the sound was coming from. The noise stopped and she heard Cinny's voice as she tapped softly on the bedroom door.

"Annie, are you busy?"

"No, come in."

The door slowly opened where Cinny was dressed in her old brittle pink crepe paper costume that had already made its announcement.

Laughing at the sudden pink paper cloud she remembered from their childhood, the sisters sat on the pink duvet covered bed and had another laugh fulfilling their promise to have a least one a day. They shared other fond memories of their childhood, and had a good laugh.

"Well, Cinny, we have had our laugh for the day thanks to you. I must say this was a total surprise. What made you think of putting that on?

"I was just browsing through the attic and saw the trunk Mum stored things like this and wondered if it was still there and it was to my surprise. She has lots of other things there I want us to explore someday together. After we had our memories of this dress I wondered if mummy kept it and she did. I hope someday I will have children and make memories like this to remember fondly as they grow up."

"She was very sentimental, opposite from Dad; he couldn't be bothered with such things as he would tell her. She made up for him though. They made a great couple; he was her strength in many ways as she was to him with hers."

"That reminds me, Annie, Matt is home. Did you know that?"

"No, no, I didn't, is he all right? No injuries or anything?"

"He's fine; Daphne said he is more handsome than ever."

"All right, all right so he is more handsome but you forget, he is three years younger than I am."

"Oh, Annie, that doesn't make any difference. He likes you. He tried to date you remember?"

"Of course I remember, how can I forget, every time I turned around he was there, he was like an irritating little brother. I could never take him seriously. He was always my 'Mattie'."

"Yes, I well remember that. He hated it when you called him that. He'd shout at you, pointing his finger at you yelling, 'My name is Matt, or Matthew, not Mattie."

They laughed remembering the name game Anise would play with him. She could never be serious with a boy three years younger than she was.

Her memories of school friends upset her with their taunting. They never ceased comments about Matt chasing her and accused her of 'robbing the cradle'.

"Annie, he is tall, blonde, big blue eyes and if I know him still has a crush on you. I hope you will give him a chance.

He was such a sweet boy, I am sure he will be a kind and loving man."

"Now little sister, don't get carried away, all I can think about when I see him is when he was in third grade and I was in sixth and how he would chase me every day on the playground. I felt like a fool. My friends used to tease me about the little boy on the playground and how he liked 'older girls'. Remember when he'd say that? Can't you remember how embarrassed I was? Those friends never let up about him. They always found something to tease me with about Matt. I tried to make a joke about it, but he was so relentless about chasing me, I couldn't keep my composure, and I'd end up making things worse and sputter something stupid each time I'd try to catch my breath and really make them laugh. No, Cinny, I don't want to talk about Matt anymore, promise?"

"Oh, all right, let's talk about our trip to London? I want to get away for a while, may we start planning our trip you promised we could take?"

"Yes, let's look at the calendar and see what we have.'

The Ladies Auxiliary' meeting it still going on because Hazel won't give them up. We have to wait until she ends them, I don't want to let her and the vicar down, they have worked so hard to help our men in uniform, so thought we should be patient until they say we can stop them or at least meet once a month or so. Besides this will be the perfect time to bring up ideas for the celebration."

"Oh, Annie, let's ask her tomorrow if we can meet once a month from now on, I so wanted to get away for at least a fortnight."

"I agree, we need to get away. I do want to find Uncle Reggie and have him start the portrait of mum and dad. We will talk to Hazel tomorrow when she comes in for her tea. How does that sound?"

"That sounds wonderful, I'm glad you agree with me. I'm tired of this place and the same thing, day after day after day....." Cinny's voice trailed off.

"Me too, we deserve a holiday and I want to do some shopping. What do you want to look for?"

"Well, I want as I told you before, to see what new clothes they have, and new cosmetics that I've heard about from the advertisements on the radio. Won't that be fun to be glamorous? I just want to feel good about myself for a change, I feel so drab and dull, don't you? I mean.... Well you know."

"I do, I understand little one, I agree it would make us feel good and hopefully find something to help us out of the old war routine, of going without, making do and mending all the time. It will feel good to splurge on a few new things."

"Happy day and, maybe I can get you away from Mattie." Cinny said running down the stairs with a head start to get away from Anise's expected chase to stop her topic of the younger man and what the future might hold.

CHAPTER SEVEN

Precisely at 7:00 pm, as customary on Wednesday evenings the members of the Ladies Auxiliary Club assembled in the village town hall that had retained its scent and flavor of 1800's England. Located across the street from the Brooker's family cottage, bakery and teashop, Captain Brooker had made a clear statement that he had built the hall as a legacy for his descendants.

Hazel Grovenor, president of the auxiliary, stood up from her usual place at the head of the large table had been built especially for them to be seated around comfortably for their meetings. It was designed to allow them ample workspace for sewing, items to be put into bags for the troops, including first aid supplies and ample room to serve their tea and cakes afterwards.

She spoke in her usual "posh" meeting voice to bring the chattering women and girls to order.

"Ladies, please be seated and let's begin our special meeting tonight. We need to have an accounting to bring to your attention all your hard work and dedication you have contributed these past war years, starting in 1939 until now.

We have sadly lost some of our members, which we will discuss at a later meeting to have memorials for them. We have added new members through the years, which we greatly appreciate their contributions and work.

Missy Odette, our treasurer, who has done a splendid job of keeping our books accurate and up to date, will read the accounting report."

"I would also like to take this time to thank you all for your hard work and dedication and loyalty to our beloved country. This report is just a summary of what was collected, used and distributed. I won't go into details, if you want more information that we don't cover this evening, please contact me or Missy and we will be most happy to show you our books."

Missy Odette, the banker's wife, stood with straight shoulders, excellent posture and well-groomed wearing her usual blue hat but without feather.

She joined Hazel at the head of the table and carefully reported all the food, baby, men, women and children, and medical kits, along with the money they had collected and the money spent. The long list went on and on, the women were getting restless, and Missy decided to end the review and turn the time back to Hazel.

"Thank you Missy, we appreciate all your careful record keeping for us. Now, we must go forward with our club activities and now it is time for you to submit ideas for future meetings for us to include and will vote on the ones you want to proceed with. I turn the time over to you, now is your chance to let us all know your ideas. I will call on you one by one, so everyone who has something to say please stand up and I will let you speak one at a time."

The ones with ideas stood up and gave their ideas for peacetime endeavors.

Anise and Cinny brought up their idea about the end of the war celebration and the hall became filled with laughter surprised and happy about their idea and agreed it would be good for the village to have something to work together on that could help give them all closure and celebrate the long trying years they had shared for the past six years.

"Do I hear 'yeas'… 'nays'? The 'yeas' have it. Good, we will start discussing committees we need to make so please nominate either yourself or someone else.

Thank you for your continuing support of our organization. It is so important for us to do for others what they cannot do for themselves, even during peacetime we will have plenty of things to keep us busy.

We will be served tea and cakes, this evening's refreshments were furnished and will be served by Daphne Shaw, of Daphne's Fashions. I shall now bless the food, so bow your heads and let us pray." Hazel said bowing her head to bless the food.

The mood grew lighter as they chatted away remembering all the things they had achieved in the past.

"I was wondering what the boys will do that have been on your farm, Irene?" Lucy Burkhart asked.

"I really don't know, they have been such a part of our family for so long, I just never thought about losing them, or that they might leave us."

"Well, I suppose they will return to London, don't they have family there? Won't they be missed by them?" Irene continued.

"We haven't asked them, since their parents were…well, killed in a bombing several years ago, we haven't had the heart to bring anything up since then. I imagine they will come to us when they want to leave. I hope they stay here."

"You have had quite a time with them, even though they are good workers. Remember the time they blackened all your sheep?" Olive Simon asked with a chuckle.

The question got everyone's attention and they all laughed at the picture of the Gates sheep the twins, Robert and Ryan Murphy had rubbed with coal dust to protect them and the location of the farm from German planes looking for a target.

"Oh, yes and the time they rigged up the line to move hay from the barn across the barnyard to the meadow where the animals would eat when suddenly the makeshift bucket whipped upside down with them in it and dumped them in the deep spring mud. They all laughed.

"Don't forget the day they had us all come to see their idea putting the milk cans on a moving board by chains they pulled and suddenly the chains started to move faster and faster until the can were flung into the air. Of course they were filled with milk.

"Yes and the time they….

The women all shared their favorite Rob and Ryan stories and nominated each other for the committees needed for the Brooker's Village-On-Sea end of the war celebration.

CHAPTER EIGHT

The Town Hall filled every Thursday night with the loyal Home Guards for one of the last meetings they would have since the Germans surrendered.

They also knew the war had not completely ended for there was still fighting in the jungles of Burma and other places which left the small squad of volunteers unsure about letting down their defenses totally and couldn't quite end their daily and nightly schedules they had been so faithful about keeping through the long duration.

"Good evening men, glad you all could come tonight to discuss when to close our Home Guard's squad. We have been reassured from Head Quarters that it is safe now to discontinue it." Tully Sherwood, the local veterinarian said with little confidence.

He was the Captain and being a large man added to his capabilities of leading the men in his squad.

He was not accepted to serve his country because of his lame leg resulting from a childhood bicycle accident which never healed properly and left him with a slight limp.

To cover his lack of confidence from years of taunting from his school mates he protected himself with a hardened shell which proved helpful in his field of taking care of all the animals in the community.

His rough exterior had been the deciding factor that the other village men thought would be best qualified for the job. They were correct and his years of service had been very satisfying to everyone in the village and felt safer because of his demeanor and large stature and the ability to take charge keep everyone under control when and if the need would arise.

"Tully, I don't feel like we should end our squad. I think we should continue until Japan has completely surrendered. The other guys feel the same way; we have already talked about it." Ron Simon said.

"Oh, you have already talked about it? Well then tell me more about your meeting." Tully said sitting down.

"We didn't have a meeting; we would talk once in a while in front of our shops that's all.

"I'm sorry, I didn't mean to sound upset, I have been thinking the same thing. I think we should continue for a while that is until Japan completely surrenders. I will call for a vote and then we can go over the schedule for the rest of this month and June. Do we have any more business tonight?"

"We need to have a village town hall meeting, the Brooker sisters want to have an end of the war celebration. I think it is a good idea, so wanted to bring it to everyone's attention." Vicar Grovenor said sitting back down.

"Yes, I agree, how about the rest of you men?"

"That is a fine idea; let me know what I can do to help." Les Corbett asked.

"Thanks Les, you need to get in touch with Hazel Grovenor, she is head of all the committees. Isn't that correct Vicar?"

"Yes, everyone that wants to help get in touch with her, she needs all the men that will volunteer."

"I wanted some ideas of what everyone was doing for your easing up of things such as the black curtains at night and when we could bring back street lighting at night?" Tully asked.

"I for one am still using my black curtains and I understand some are not, but I agree with Tully until Japan has surrendered I don't feel comfortable being a sitting duck for them." Phil Gates chuckled. "I took mine down but I thought about putting them back up...I am just not sure." Frank Jarvis said.

"All I can say is make your own decision and in time we will know what to do or not do...it won't be overnight that we can feel free to have a normal routine in our new situation of war's end." Tully said thoughtfully.

"I agree, if we feel strong about something we need to continue and if not we can stop, it is as simple as that. Time will tell. It will take some time to purge ourselves of six years of war routines." Richard Grovenor said.

"Well, men, you can see the new schedule in the hallway so if anyone can't fill their spot, let me know. If there is no other matter, this meeting is closed and will see you next week." Tully said dismissing everyone.

He walked to his home in back of his veterinary building.

CHAPTER NINE

Matthew Rutledge brought the large storage boxes into the small crowded antiques shop his father couldn't wait to hand down to him. He wasn't overjoyed to think he would be spending the rest of his life as proprietor.

Since his mother passed away before he returned home he found his father couldn't work there any longer and was not able to overcome the sadness of losing his most beloved wife. Everything reminded him of her. Each item in the shop had a history of her one way or the other.

When Matt arrived home from his four year tour of service in the RAF he was surprised to find his father had fallen apart from the death of his mother.

The day Matt returned home and had a welcome home dinner the father left for Cornwall, the very next day.

His memories of his parents were happy ones and he always looked up to them and their work esthetics.

They were kind and loving to him and his older brother and younger sister they all three had fond memories they shared on his return from France.

Matt decided to make the best of his homecoming and become a shop owner even though it would be short lived if he had his way about it.

His siblings would not consider taking the family business and so it fell to him to keep the shop open for his mourning father and allowed him to leave.

Silently he hoped if he could make it more successful he would convince them to sell it and he could then get on with the life he dreamed of which was to build boats.

This had been a complete change from his childhood plans to go into the aviation field.

Thoughts of his childhood ran through his mind when he and his friends would sit in the movies on Saturday afternoons washed over him that day. His favorite ones were about air planes. He became enamored with the Red Baron from the First World War.

A twist of fate he met a boat builder in the south of France. The old Frenchman took him on his first sailboat ride and he was enthralled with the feel of the boat skimming across the waves. He knew then he had to watch the process of making boats when he had a chance to get back there.

The next project he dreamed of was the lovely Anise Brooker.

He had loved her all his life. She never once gave him hope there was any chance he could win her over. She would only laugh at him and call him Mattie and run away. Anise would always make it clear he was too young for her but he promised himself he would change her mind someday and she would fall in love with him as he was with her.

He smiled remembering one day when she came into the shop looking for a lamp for her room.

He couldn't believe his luck that it was he who had the honor of waiting on her. He went through every corner he could find to bring out all they had. To his great surprise she actually bought a pair. He was thrilled. With a shaking hand wrote out a receipt for her and gave it to her stammering 'I hope this will light up your room as you light up a room when you enter.'

He would never forget what he said and berated himself every day since for sounding so silly and must have looked that way as well.

He reminded himself how he was never the poetic type and just be himself.

His plan was to clear out anything he didn't like or thought wouldn't sell. He would take a trip to London and find new inventory. Before the trip he would clean and paint and organize in a way that would attract customers. He remembered some of the shops in France he went into and enjoyed browsing around and had actually sent some things home to his family.

He and Collin Jarvis, his best friend was to meet for dinner at the 'Beach Front Café' that evening.

Collin had also just returned from France where he was also in the RAF stationed there. They were very surprised when they found they were both stationed at the same aerodrome.

Collin was a pharmacist in his father's 'Jarvis Chemist' store, down the street from his 'Rutledge Antiques' shop.

The friends started going to the 'Home Guard' meetings to support the old guys and the young ones who had not been able to serve their country during the war.

They tried to convince the village squad it was time to end the group, but had not been able to reassure them there would be no need for their guarding the community any longer.

Completing the packing of odds and ends into the cartons he carried them to the storage part of the business in the back of the store.

He turned on the small light left on overnight for security purposes and locked up shop and walked down to meet Collin.

"Hi Matt, be with you in just a minute, I have to finish my totals for the day before Ivy comes to take her shift."

"Did your father retire?"

"Not yet, but he is well on his way."

"I'll just look around while you finish."

Matt slowly meandered down the aisles to see what they had to sell when he spotted Anise and Cinny on the next one.

"What are you two doing here?"

"We are playing Rugby can't you see?" Anise said.

"Well, I see you haven't changed since I've been away." He chuckled.

"I see you haven't either, still the same old Mattie." She laughed knowing he would get mad at her.

"How are you Cinny, you look well?"

"I am doing well, you look good too."

"Now that is settled let's get going we have lots to do before we leave for London." Anise said wanting to move away from the uncomfortable feeling she had seeing him for the first time in four years and recognizing he was more handsome than ever.

"You are going to London, when?"

"Tomorrow, why?"

"I might see you; I am going as well tomorrow. I have to buy some inventory for the shop. Are you going to see your Uncle, the one with the art shop?"

"Yes, we are, why?"

"Nothing, just wondered." He would be going to London tomorrow and find them at the shop if he would be lucky enough to time it just right. He felt his luck was changing with Miss Brooker and noticed a tiny bit of warmth coming from her.

Whistling softly he returned to his friend to leave to have dinner and talk about old times and compare experiences of the last four years.

The last of the orange sun melted into the darkening sky caught by the smooth water of the English Channel.

The two friends shared their experiences

Of the past four years, both good and bad. They agreed it would take some time to get back into normal life and that their lives would never be the same.

"Matt, do you still like Anise?"

"Yes, more than ever, I know she is the one I want to spend the rest of my life with. I have never given up on her and know someday she will feel the same way about me as I do her."

"Are you sure you are not wasting your time? I didn't think she was too happy to see you in the shop just now."

"I know you couldn't see or feel it, but I felt a ting of warmth coming from her for the first time. I know it will take some time and maneuvering but I am going to do it."

"I suppose you know what you are doing, I wish you well."

"What about you?"

"I think about Cinny quite a bit lately, since I have been home that is. She has matured into a beautiful young woman since I left. Don't you agree?"

"Yes, she has, beautiful like her older sister. We just need to hang in there and see what we can do to help things along. I am going to London tomorrow and try to catch up with them, want to go with me?"

"Sure, I'll get Ivy to take my shift. She loves to work; I think she does it to keep her mind and thoughts off Darrel's death. It is sad, as you know they were only married a couple of years before he left.

She never complains though."

"Maybe we can cheer her up, find someone for her to go with, she needs to get out once in a while."

"I agree, let's do that soon. Let's order, I am starved."

CHAPTER TEN

Hazel slowly walked up the hill of the High Street to the Brooker's Bakery, with thoughts of how she could help Les and maybe even Nigel stop drinking.

She agreed with her husband that sooner or later something terrible would inescapability happen and she wanted to prevent it if possible.

She felt the village had survived the war and now was the time to look forward to good times.

She decided to stop at the bakery and buy a fresh loaf of bread to add to the fruit basket she was going to fill from the Simpson's Grocery for Les to give her an excuse to talk to him and maybe implement and go forward with an idea of how to save him from himself.

"Good morning Hazel, how are you this morning?"

"I am doing very well, thank you. I shall have two loaves of your wonderful French bread. I think I will take some cinnamon buns home for Richard, he loves them with his tea."

"Do we have all the committees we need for the celebration?"

"Almost, we only need more to volunteer to help decorate the day before; will you help out with that, you and Cinny?"

"Yes, of course, let us know who is in charge and we will contact them. Did you need anything else?"

"No dear, that will be all, put it on our account. By the way, you have the understanding we will order the food from you as soon as they have completed their list I will give it to you so your staff will be ready to prepare it. We will raise the money to pay for it with some sidewalk bake sales and other ideas they come up with. So we will need an estimate as soon as you receive the list."

"Of course, and you have a great day. You know, I have never thanked you for all you do in the village. It seems when we need help you are there. Oh, by the way, Matt Rutledge is head of the decorating committee."

"Oh, he is? That sounds odd to have a man; I mean…well, we can help it needed. We just all need to work together.

I think the war brought us all closer together, don't you think?"

"I do, we did get something good from it."

"Good bye for now, and you have a great day as well."

Hazel continued her walk back down the hill stopping at the Chemist for some headache tablets.

"Hello Ivy, how are you today?"

"I am doing very well Hazel, and how are you?" "I am very well. I need some tablets for headaches."

"Sure, over here." She said handing her the bottle.

"Thank you and put it on our account."

"Certainly." She said as she made note of it and walked her to the door.

All of the sudden they heard a woman yelling and saw it was Olive chasing Ron down the street with a broom.

"I wish she wouldn't do that, it seems extreme and they should keep their problems behind closed doors." Hazel winced.

"I know, I think he enjoys it or he wouldn't do things in front of her." "I thought about that as well, do you think he is doing those flirtations on purpose to see her get mad?"

"I heard he told someone he wanted a little "grit" in his marriage."

"Well, he has it and much more. I wonder if she has any idea about this." Hazel asked.

"I don't know but I am going to find out. I am going to take her to lunch and find out."

"Good, it is about time and please let me know what she says."

"I will but don't tell anyone." Ivy said.

"I promise and I will see you later. Good bye."

"Good bye."

Hazel continued the walk to her destination' Les' Tailor Shop', where she found him washing outside windows.

"Hello Les, I brought you a basket of fruit and a loaf of fresh bread from Brooker's. I understand that is your favorite."

"Thank you Hazel, that is so kind of you. How are you doing?"

"I am well, may I come in and sit down for a few minutes, and I am tired."

"Please come in, may I bring you a cup of tea?"

"That would be so nice, I could use some tea."

"Have you and the ladies organized the village end of the war celebration?"

"Almost, we have some loose ends but most committees are ready to go to work."

"Is there anything I can do to help?"

"Yes, Matt and Collin need help with the art work for the decorations and asked me to ask you and Nigel. Also will you both take pictures for us? I know you recently bought a new camera and thought you would enjoy taking them for us."

"Yes, I would love to do the photos for the celebration. That has become my hobby and I find it gives me great pleasure."

"Wonderful, that is settled and how would you like to come for dinner some night with Richard and I?" "Well, I will check my schedule."

"Les, are you trying to get out of it?"

"Well, sometimes I have headaches and have to go home and go to bed early."

"Les, may I ask you a personal question?"

"Maybe, depends on what question."

"Why do you persist in this drinking business, you and Nigel?"

"I don't know, I guess it is a…well…a…I don't know. It just happens, I can feel low and it helps me feel good."

"Have you tried to not let it just happen?"

"Not really why?"

"I am worried someday something bad will happen to you and to Nigel if you don't stop. You know God gives us chances to correct our lives on our own and if we don't He will do the correcting and it isn't always pleasant."

"What do you mean not pleasant?"

"You read the Bible?"

"Well, I used to, it has been awhile."

"You need to read the Bible; there is a lot of good advice in it. There are many places we are warned about strong drink."

"I will read it, someday when I have some time. My business has really gotten out of hand with all the men returning home from the war. They all want new suits. So when I can I will, and thank you Hazel for caring. I know you are kind and mean well."

"Wonderful and I do care and please talk about this with Nigel."

"I will, tonight."

"Thank you for the tea and I must go and let me know if you need my help."

"I promise and have a good day." He said wanting to get rid of her and her inquiring personal questions.

Hazel felt good about her visit and that she had made progress in her first attempt to help Les and Nigel stop drinking.

CHAPTER ELEVEN

"Well, Cinny, are you ready for this?" Anise asked clicking her suitcase shut.

"Yes, I was ready last night; did you give Audrey the list of daily chores?"

"I did that yesterday on our lunch break. Polly and the others are on call on their day off; we can phone every day to check on them. I am not worried we will only be gone a few days. I want to get away for a while, Uncle Reggie is happy we are coming and is excited about the portrait, I have our photo just in case he doesn't have the one I wanted him to use for the portrait."

"You drive for a while and I will drive into London, ok?" Anise asked.

"That is the best way, I have never driven in London, and I don't want to start now. I can always do that later when I am in the mood. Ah ha…" In the Mood", the song…funny huh? I am a poet and you didn't even know it did you?" Cinny laughed.

"Let's go, Shakespeare."

Driving the narrow winding countryside roads were an enjoyable change for the sisters as the smooth humming of the motor of the older but well taken care of the light blue M G carried them swiftly to their destination.

"I can't believe we are here, I must have gone to sleep." Cinny yawned.

"You did sleep, I was afraid I would get sleepy but I didn't, for some reason."

"I know why, you were thinking about meeting Matt. I know he will find out where we are and will be there."

"You must have been dreaming, I was not, only thinking about our future."

"Don't lie, Annie, it's just me, you can be honest with your feelings about him. I promise I will never tell anyone anything you tell me in confidence. You know you can trust me."

"I know, but you better not ever…and yes, I was thinking about him. I couldn't believe my feelings when I saw him with Collin in the shop. Matt looked so handsome. I had forgotten how tall he is. Do you think he grew taller during the war?"

"He might have, but he has always been tall and good looking. Thank you for opening up, you know we are more than sisters, we are best friends, and well you are my best friend anyway." Cinny smiled.

"You are my best friend too little one."

"I don't enjoy this traffic it is bumper to bumper and the exhaust from the red double decker buses is beginning to make my throat dry. Can you feel it too?"

"Yes, I always go home with a sore throat. Here we are, I can't believe there is a parking space. We are taking the bus while we are here and leave the car parked. Let's get our cases."

The 'Brooker's Art' shop hadn't changed in over thirty years. The old brick facing appeared even more faded but, the large bay window was spotless to display Reggie Brooker's paintings.

Passersby would continuously stop and admire the artist's work and many entered to purchase one that caught their attention.

He could never fill all his orders as they overlapped in purchases and future orders, which made him happy.

Reginald Brooker was the younger brother of the girl's father. He was short and slightly on the heavy side. His thick brown hair was usually uncombed but clean. His average looks helped him to submerge into his art making his non-descript appearance a gift in itself.

His wife Lily was small but lovely in frame, as he would say and would use her from time to time in his paintings dressing her up in several old world style costumes.

Her short gray hair didn't take away from her blue eyes and large eyeglasses.

"My goodness you girls are stunning. I have to do a portrait of you both, will you sit for me while you are here?" He said opening the door.

"I don't know if we have time we will, can't you take our picture and do it from that?" Anise asked while sitting her luggage down to hug her favorite uncle.

"I suppose so, but please stay as long as you can. I miss you so much."

He led them to their large bedroom with two beds and the usual fireplace.

He had cleaners come in and put it in perfect order for his nieces.

The bright paisley print of the duvet's and curtains added the touch he wanted to have the room as comfortable and enjoyable as possible.

The crystal bedside water pitchers by the bronze lamps emphasized the large mahogany tables beside each bed.

"I hope you will be able to sleep and be comfortable while you are here. Mrs. Madison will see to it you want for nothing. I may have to miss some meals but she will be able to have your meals on time. You just give her what you want and when each morning for the day."

"Thank you, everything looks great, so fresh and clean and the fresh roses are wonderful."

"Why don't you sell your shop here and move to the village and live with us?"

"I never thought about that, I thought maybe you would move here. I will think about it, I wouldn't mind getting out of town."

"We are having an 'end of the war' celebration; will you and Aunt Lily come?"

"Let me check with her first but I think we may be able to do that, and then we will see what transpires, by the way, Matt Rutledge phoned and gave me his phone number to let him know where you girls go shopping. He wants to take you to dinner. Is it all right if I call him, or better yet, will you phone him and let him know where you will be? He is a nice young man. He also has his friend, Collin Jarvis with him; they are staying with some friends from university."

"Yes, we will phone them, we knew they would be here. Do you know when you will be busy for dinner so we won't miss having dinner with you?"

"I have a sitting tomorrow night, so maybe you could make a date with them then?"

"That will work; we will make sure Mrs. Madison knows our schedule." Anise said winking at Cinny.

The small dining room's ivory walls reflected the candles placed carefully on the antique family table and because of its size was used only for company. Everyday meals were eaten in the kitchen by the large window overlooking the back garden.

"We have dinner ready so freshen up and we will eat."

Anise and Cinny washed their faces and brushed their hair in the bedroom's unsuited bathroom.

"Well, Matt didn't lose any time contacting Uncle Reggie did he?" Cinny chuckled.

"I was surprised at his tenacity. He meant what he said didn't he?"

"He has always been persistent, you have never noticed."

"I tried for years to ignore him; this is an odd feeling to actually agree to have dinner with him. I hope I don't make a fool out of myself. Please help me remain calm will you?"

"Of course I will come to your rescue if I need to. You may be surprised and have a good evening talking and actually getting acquainted. You don't even know what he likes and dislikes."

"I am going to remember what you've just said and maybe it will make me ask him questions and take the pressure off me."

"Yes, picture him the little Mattie from school and that should make you smile and relax."

"That is a good idea little Cinnamon, that will make me feel at ease I am sure. I will picture him on the playground turning cartwheels to impress me and my friends. We would laugh at him and go inside to our classes."

"That is a good idea, but tomorrow night you will see just how much that little boy turning cartwheels has grown into a very handsome young man." Cinny smiled at her sister.

CHAPTER TWELVE

The slow rocking waves drew the sun's warm rays into its cradles.

Matt and Collin threw small pebbles in to park's pond that launched the ducks, geese, and swans into the air.

Laughing at their unintended disturbance they sat on a black iron bench in front of the large green pine trees.

"I always thought I would go into the aviation field when I returned home but I got side tracked into sailing.

I had a few days off and I borrowed one of the guys' small car and traveled to southern France where I came upon a village quite like our own.

I spotted a man working on a boat that was turned upside down and he was sanding it carefully to make it as smooth as possible. I noticed how he bent down as close as he could to see the results.

I found a rock nearby to sit on and watched him for a long time and then he walked over to me and asked me in broken English, if I had ever sailed. I told him no.

He invited me to go out with him on a new boat he had just finished and needed to see how it sailed. I at first was concerned he might be the enemy, for we had just liberated France and not everyone was our friend. But then I had the feeling he was safe. Besides, I was younger and stronger and could take him if I had to.

Anyway to make a long story short, I loved it…we skimmed along it seemed on top of the water and it was an incredible feeling I had never had before."

"So you are thinking you will go into the boat business?"

"Yes, I am, and I am going to take Anise there on our honeymoon and be an apprentice for about a year and come back home and open my own business."

"That sounds like a final deal…only one flaw…Anise." Collin laughed.

"Yes, that could take some time, but in the mean time I will save as much money as I can so it won't be wasted time waiting for her to come around."

"I wish I had my life planned. I am going to just fade away in the pharmacy shop."

"Haven't you ever thought about doing something other than the pharmacy?"

"Yes, I have, but father wants Ivy and me to take the business so he can retire."

"What do you want to do if you had the opportunity?"

"I would like to go back to university and become a doctor. When I was in the service I had the chance to help the doctors once in a while when they were shorthanded. I got to observe up close everything they did and I wanted to be more useful but wasn't. I would day dream about going back to school and becoming one. Then I remember father and how he would look if I told him I didn't want the chemist shop."

"Couldn't you work up to it, like ask questions about Ivy and if she could handle it by herself and maybe get her a partner?"

"I hadn't thought about it that way, I could lead up to it. I will, I am going to do it. What did your father say about you not having his shop any longer?"

"I haven't told him yet, but it is time I did. I am going to take a trip to Cornwall when we get home, I'll have Jeremy take over while I am gone, he is honest and a good worker. He might even be interested in buying father out."

"Well, we have it all settled, then don't we?"

"It looks that way. All we have to do is pray all goes well. Let's go find the girls, Reggie said they would be at the dress shop by two o'clock and it is half past one now."

"I don't like ladies dress shops, I am always afraid I am going to see something I shouldn't."

"You are so funny; we aren't going to see anything but some old ladies trying on clothes too tight for them. That is all I had ever seen when I went in with mother years ago."

The small dress shop was warm from the sunlit windows so the door was opened to bring some fresh air in and circulate around the crowded racks.

"There they are, Cinny is sitting there and looks like Anise is trying on a dress for her. Let's hide over here."

Matt whispered slipping into a darkened corner.

"Oh, look over there at that big lady" Collin nudged Matt.

"Good grief, she is spilling out all over that strapless red dress. That is awful." Matt said turning his head.

"I told you, I told you we would see something we shouldn't see."

"Shhhh, be quiet. Let's tip toe over to the girls."

"What are you doing here?" Anise asked blushing.

"We came to ask you both out for dinner."

"What are you staring at Collin?"

"Oh, nothing, just the dresses." He blushed this time.

"We will pick you up at six o'clock, is that all right?" "Yes, that will be fine, see you then." Cinny said.

The two young men quickly walked out of the warm women's clothing shop silently vowing never to enter one again.

"What did I tell you Matt?"

"I know you warned me but I have never been so embarrassed in my whole life. I thought that woman was going to burst that dress and have red pieces of fabric all over the shop. It must have been sewed with iron thread and had metal weaved through the fabric for it not to have come completely apart."

"Let's go have a cold drink and relax before we get ready to pick up them up."

Matt escorted Anise, Cinny and Collin to the reserved table in the quiet place he had asked for. He wanted to have some relaxed conversation and enjoy being together away from home. His ultimate goal was to melt Anise's heart to allow him to ask her out on dates when they returned home.

"This is nice; I like the green foliage that separates the tables for privacy." Cinny said.

"How did your shopping go after we left?"

"Very well, it took some time but we found some bargains there and another store." Anise replied.

"Uh, did you happen to see the…uh…lady trying on the red dress?" Collin asked clearing his throat.

"You mean the one that looked like it was going to burst at the seams?"

"Yes, that is the one."

"She came out of the dressing room just as you came up to us. I was hoping you hadn't seen her for her sake. That was so embarrassing." Cinny shook her head.

"I can't believe she would even leave the dressing room to let anyone see what she looked like." Anise winced.

"I thought the same thing…why would anyone go out in public that way? I feel for her poor husband" Matt started to chuckle.

"That was bad enough but she was twirling around and around, all I could think of was please don't rip the seams." Collin laughed.

"Not only that but she was overflowing the top as well. It was all I could do not to put my hands over my eyes." Anise laughed.

They all four laughed more and more as the image came back to them one, depicting something the other hadn't until they all four had to excuse themselves and go outside until they got themselves under control and go back inside and order their meal.

The red dress incident had broken the ice and gave Anise the chance to soften her heart towards Matt. and he could tell she was allowing him to come closer.

CHAPTER THIRTEEN

Les rolled the tall ladder outside in front of the large window of his shop kicking the safety catch into place so it wouldn't roll while he was cleaning.

He hated the climb up and up to the top to do the chore he detested. Not only the height of the ladder but the inevitable streaks he would notice when he would climb down thinking the job was completed, go back inside and would detect his imperfect job.

The month before he found if he took a couple of drinks before he started the dreaded task it went much nicer and he even hummed as he started to wipe it clean.

After he had everything in place including the pre cleaning drinks began his chore reaching as far as he could with an upward circular motion.

Suddenly, he felt the ladder leap as the catch flew open and he and the ladder began to move down the hill, gradually gaining momentum until he felt as though he was flying and becoming aware he was sailing closer and closer to the churchyard.

Without warning the ladder struck a small rock lifting him and the wheeled object into the air throwing him up and over the stone wall and landed directly onto the verdant lawn of the vicarage in a fetal position.

"Les, are you all right?" Hazel whispered to the man lying face down on her green grass.

"Hazel, I think he is unconscious." Richard said.

"Phone the doctor quickly, I will stay here with him."

Dr. Burkhart had the bystanders help him lift Les onto a gurney and carry his unconscious friend into the spare bedroom of the vicarage.

"We need to get him to the hospital if he doesn't come around soon. I will phone and have they prepare for his possible admittance."

While they were talking Les blinked open his eyes and asked "Where am I?"

"You had an accident Les, you are here in our spare bedroom, how do you feel?"

"I don't know, what should I be feeling? What happened?"

"You took a wild ride on your ladder and landed on the lawn." Hazel said placing a cold cloth on his forehead.

"Oh, yes, I remember now." Les went silent and closed his eyes.

"All right, you can all go home now, he is going to be fine and thank you for your help and concern. Please don't share this with anyone." Hazel whispered as she took the by standers outside of the room and closed the door so Les wouldn't be able to hear her conversation and plea not to repeat what had happened.

"We won't say anything Hazel" They whispered back to her as they left.

"George is he all right or should he go to the hospital?"

Richard asked.

"No, I think he is all right, I checked for broken bones and he doesn't seem to have a temperature that would indicate anything so far. I want to see if he can walk before I leave. He's been drinking."

"I was afraid of that. Les, do you think you can get up and walk before I leave? You don't have any broken bones that is amazing, you are a very fortunate man, someone was watching over you." "Yes, I am grateful, I want to go home. Will you take me in your car?"

"I will, but let's see how you do getting out of bed and tell me if you have pain anywhere."

Les slowly slid his legs over the side of the bed and pushed himself up on his shaking legs.

"Don't move just stand there and let me see how you do and if you are dizzy. I think you should stay here with Hazel and Richard at least for the night."

"I am fine, just shaky. I want to go home and besides my store is still open."

"We phoned Tully and he is there is now."

"Thank you, I will be fine now. I just need to go home and take a hot shower and get some sleep."

"You seem to be fine, since you don't have any broken bones; I am surprised you didn't with the magnitude of the fall. You will be sore tomorrow though, so be prepared you will have some pain when you wake up."

"I will be fine. I want to go home."

"Come on, I will get you there, walk slowly to my car."

"I will bring you breakfast in the morning at nine, is that too late?" Hazel asked.

"That would be all right I'll see then." He said as he slowly walked to the waiting car.

The morning sun illuminated the streaked window Les had started to wash the fateful day before.

He rubbed his throbbing temples. The dreaded headache hadn't gone away with the tablets Dr. Burkhart left for him to take the night before.

Taking a deep breath he slowly finished dressing after his long shower to help him try to calm his aching body from the humiliating fall on the vicarage lawn in front of half the village.

With shaking hands he brushed his thick graying hair that added to his handsome face which drinking to excess hadn't diminished his good looks.

He rode his bicycle as much as he could to get some exercise and he found it made him feel better to work up a sweat.

Staring into the oval mirror in the bathroom he designed a few years ago to make sure he could see if he coordinated his attire properly for the day.

He could hear the shop bell alerting him there was someone coming into the shop and slowly went downstairs to face the dreaded day.

"Hazel, thank you for coming and I am prepared for your sermon." He smiled sheepishly taking the breakfast basket.

"Let's sit at the table. I have made some notes for you to remember each day. You open one each day and I will bring more as time goes on. I don't want you to feel alone. I think that could be part of your problem"

"I don't know about that but the notes are fine and I will read them. I know you are right, I have to quit drinking. When I went flying down the street yelling 'help' I knew that was my last drinking day. I promised God if I lived through it I would stop."

"I can't tell you how happy it makes me feel for you to say that. We all reach the point in our lives when we need to change and that God will always help us, He is always there, that is if we allow Him to come into our life. Remember you are not alone. We, everyone in the village, and the world have something to work on, yours is more obvious than some of ours."

"I never thought about it that way. Thank you and I am looking forward to the notes. You are a good friend, Hazel. If there is ever anything I can do for you, please let me know."

"That won't be necessary, but if something comes up I will.

I will see you in the morning with another basket, so if you need me before then call or come over."

"I will and thank you again and I will see you in the morning."

Les dialed Nigel to share with him the start of the new phase of his life and for him to join him in the long process of going without alcohol that they had each talked about in the past, but not seriously until now.

CHAPTER FOURTEEN

Blue smoke billowed out from the windows, doors and cracks of the make shift tin building the Murphy brothers had built a few years ago with odds and ends from the local junkyard on the far end of the field but plain view of the large farm house.

Phil and Irene Gates had wanted to allow them a place they could call their own to pursue their inventions that would pop up every once in a while without getting into Phil's workshop and 'not blow it up' as he shared with his wife from experiences with them from the past.

"Rob, are you all right, I can't see you?" The older brother asked trying to clear the smoke fanning a large piece of cardboard.

"I'm fine; I just don't understand why we can't get these instructions down so we don't have this premature explosion."

"I know, me too, what are we not doing properly …or overlooking?"

"I was hoping you would know because I sure don't."

"Are you guys all right?" Homer Adams, their co-worker and friend asked running into the smoky building.

"Yes, we are fine, just can't understand what we are doing wrong." Ryan said rubbing his eyes.

"Why don't we take the instructions to the professor at the university in Wolford?"

"You mean Mr. Cunningham?"

"Yes, remember he said he would help us when we needed it and feel free to call him and make an appointment."

"You are right, let's go phone him and see how soon we can see him and find out what is going on." Ryan said.

The Gates family watched from the kitchen window to see if the boys were all right. The young men and women from London that were placed on their farm became part of their family and to Wesley and Marilee Phil and Irene's ten year old son and twelve year old daughter as their siblings.

"Well, I see Tweedledum and Tweedledee are at it again." Marilee laughed.

"Yeah, they are more fun than the movies on Saturday." Wesley chuckled.

He was a quiet and reserved boy and allowed Marilee the privilege to always be in charge. He was very studious and meticulous which made it hard for him to identify with the usually grimy older boys.

"What did I tell you about your sarcastic remarks about the boys?" Irene asked.

"You said not to be so sarcastic." Marilee retorted.

Marilee was twelve years old going on twenty, or so she thought.

She was tall for her age with long brown hair and blue eyes that never missed anything in range.

She walked as though she was in complete control and knew exactly where she was going and what she was doing including the habit of swinging her hair to one side out of her pretty face when she was stressed, upset or trying to get her way about something.

"I promise you little miss, if you or your brother makes one more smart remark about the boys or girls you will not have the privilege of going shopping on Saturday mornings ever again. You both will stay home and do chores."

"Oh, all right, but they make it so easy mum how can we stop?" Marilee asked with her usual smirk.

"Young lady, all you have to do is take a deep breath and leave the situation if you feel you can't control your tongue, just clear your throat or cough, anything to stop the words from coming out. Whatever works for you, I am not joking with you. These boys have lost their families in the blitz and they will not suffer any more pain from you, do you understand what I am saying?"

"Yes, I'm sorry." Wesley said.

"Me too." Marilee echoed holding her head down.

"Now, let's go see if there is something we can do to help them clean up. They are always helping us."

The family walked together to the old shed and through the door and found the boys sitting at the drawing board they had made themselves. Irene had found some bar stools she recovered the seats so they could be comfortable doing their most favorite hobby, drawing their inventions on large pieces of paper.

"Are you boys all right?" Phil asked.

"Yes, we are fine and are going to get some help from Professor Cunningham we made an appointment with him tomorrow. We need to find out what we are doing wrong. We can't figure out what is missing." Ryan said scratching his head.

Marilee started to cough and ran out of the building.

"Wonder what that was all about?" Rob asked.

"She is allergic to smoke, she is very sensitive." Irene smiled and said covering up for her daughter knowing why she had to run out of the situation and very pleased with the results of the scolding she had just given her.

"If you need any help with this let us know, take your time but be sure your main chores are done." Phil said.

"Do you need help?" Wesley asked.

"We will, if you are able meet us here in the morning and go over the help we need and we really appreciate it that is very thoughtful." Ryan said.

Walking arm in arm back to the house, Phil and Irene talked about the list they had to do to help with the celebration and Irene revealed the reason Marilee made such a hasty retreat.

"Do you think we can convince Rob and Ryan and even Homer to stay here with us?" Irene asked.

"I was wondering the same thing, and was thinking about getting some help and build them a cottage in front of the shed."

"That would be wonderful, what a good idea, their own cottage. If you tell them that it might convince them we truly want them to stay and be part of the family. Not only to help around the farm but later on if they wanted to go to university. They need to get their inquiring minds educated." Irene laughed thinking about what Marilee was doing at that moment.

"They have become part of our family haven't they?"

"Yes, they have, they are good hearted boys and will make good husbands, this goes for Homer."

"Yes, Homer as well. He is so quiet I forget about him."

CHAPTER FIFTEEN

The shop window reflected the afternoon sun into the well-organized up to date men's clothing shop.

Les refolded some of the white shirts customer's had rifled through earlier in the day.

Waiting for his best friend Nigel to meet him for an early dinner he decided to make a phone order for some new fabric he needed for a new three piece suite for the vicar. He wanted to repay him and Hazel for being such good friends and help him hold onto some self-respect after his wild ride on the ladder a few days before.

"Nigel, glad you are here, I need you to help me measure my shop, I want to order some new suit racks I saw in an advertisement."

"Sure, how are you feeling?"

"Better, I am going to get through this episode. First of all I am going to stay as busy as I can. I have new projects to do and we have to start practicing our chamber music we are playing for the celebration. You need a new suit."

"You sound in control. Yes, I do need a new suit. I need to tell you though; I am not on the wagon as you are. I don't have the extreme problem you do." "Really?"

"Yes, really."

"Let me refresh your memory. O.K. now remember the night we both got stuck in the tree outside the town hall?"

"Yes, I remember that."

"How did we get down?"

"They had to call for the fire truck with the long ladder."

"Why did we get stuck in the tree?"

"I don't remember."

"Why don't you remember?"

"I…well…we had a few drinks."

"Now, what about the time we were stranded way out in the Channel?"

"What about it?"

"Why were we stranded way out in the Channel?"

"I think we made a bet we could go from the village harbor to France in three hours in my boat."

"Yes, we did make a bet with someone, I can't remember who, and how did we get back home?"

"The home guards had to come after us."

"Was that embarrassing?"

"Was it ever?"

"Why did we do that silly bet?"

"We had been drinking."

"How long did it take to live that one down?"

"Months if I remember correctly."

"Yes, it was close to a year."

"What about the time you were hiding in the bushes in the park with camouflage leaves and flowers glued all over and jumped out scaring a young couple walking with a small child and frightened them to death. The child could not be quieted down even after you pulled off all the leaves and flowers. What happened when the police came?"

"They said I was drunk and disorderly and took me to jail."

"What about the time we were propped up on the hill overlooking the church and we aimed our old riffles at the people coming out of the church that Sunday morning. The vicar had to make us come down before the police would come from all the commotion of the congregation."

"What had we been doing just before we went up there?"

"Drinking, all right, all right, I see your point. I still don't know if I am going to stop drinking. That is the only thing that makes me feel happy. Otherwise I will have nothing to help me feel better."

"How long have you wanted to give music lessons?"

"For years."

"Why haven't you?"

"No one will trust their children with me."

"Why is that?"

"Because I drink."

"If you stop drinking now, I promise you it won't be long and the village will know it and they will be able to trust you."

"Why are you all of a sudden this nondrinker?"

"Because on that out of control ride down to the vicarage my life actually passed before my eyes and I saw myself as this old town drunk that was the joke of many conversations. I promised God that I would quit drinking, that is why. I don't want us to be the butt of jokes any longer; it is time we grew up. We are not getting any younger, you know."

"I know, O.K. I will try it. Will you help me?"

"Certainly, Hazel will help us both. We need someone to report to, you know, like when we were in the service and was given a job to do we had to report when we completed it."

"She isn't too fond of me; I don't think she will want to help me too."

"Why isn't she fond of you?"

"I called her Hazel the witch a few times when I was drunk."

"What else?"

"Well, I asked Richard how he could stand to be married to her."

"Where were you when you asked him that?"

"Sunday morning service."

"How did you ask him that?"

"I stood up in the congregation when he was giving his sermon about loving everyone."

"Were you sober?"

"No, I had some very nice champagne for breakfast."

"Yeah, more champagne than breakfast."

"O.K. …O.K. I get the message; I have a lot of apologizing to do. I just don't know how I can get through this, you will have to baby sit me, that's it, I'll hire a babysitter. An old one, so I won't be called a… well, you know what I mean."

"I know, I guess I will take it one step at a time. One day at a time." Les said.

"Yeah, one day at a time."

"So, will you so with me when I visit with Hazel and the Vicar?"

"Yes, I suppose there is no other way. I do want to feel better about myself. It is time I grew up and let the war go and not let that be my excuse for ruining my life. Since I retired from my job the Housing Counsel's office I have been lost. They did put up with me when they didn't have to; I have to start there to make amends. It is going to take a long time to do this. But I have the time. Who knows maybe after they see, I mean the village, and maybe they will allow me to teach music to their children. I am going to start with the Gates, children. Marilee and Wesley show interest."

"I'll go with you out to their farm if you want."

"Yes, please, I'll phone them and set up a time and let you know."

"Let's go practice. We need to select our music repertoire for the celebration." Les said patting his old friend on the shoulder and happy to have a friend to go him through the dreaded days ahead.

CHAPTER SIXTEEN

Ivy locked the door to the family chemist shop and walked slowly to the back and opened the door to the storage room where she had spent many hours alone practicing her guitar.

Her mother would bring her to work when she was a child and therefore her father's shop had been her playground, hideaway and job after graduating from university with a degree as a pharmacist.

Her brief two year marriage to her childhood sweetheart, Darryl, left deep wounds next to the ones for her mother.

When she turned thirty five two months ago she could feel herself go into a deep depression and she couldn't find a way out. All she had in her thoughts were old maid, spinster and no children.

In order to get through all the dark days she would practice her guitar singing the latest hits and also play her favorite classical Chopin, Mozart, Debussy and Bach music from her music classes at university.

She had found these lone sessions helped her overcome at least for a few hours a night her pain of having been married to Darryl, her sweetheart through their teen years, for only two years before he went overseas.

Sipping a glass of water she cleared her throat, took a deep breath and began to sing her favorite song, "Reflections".

She had been overwhelmed when she heard it on the radio. She would sing out as loud as she could trying to imitate what she had heard that had engrained her heart, thoughts and feelings of perfect emotions concerning the loss of her love and had ended up with an empty life.

Without her knowledge, Tully let himself in the back of the chemist shop with his own key they had made for him years ago to get his meds for the animals they would order for him. He was later than usual and hurriedly went back behind the counter to find his package.

Suddenly he heard this beautiful sound of someone singing and stood still to listen where it was coming from and if Ivy and Collin had left the radio on and he would turn it off.

He opened the door to the storage room and was stunned to see Ivy sitting there with the guitar in her lap and singing and then when seeing him stopped.

"Tully, what are you doing here?" She blurted out.

"I was just going to ask you the same thing, was that you singing just now?"

"Yes, it was until you scared the holy daylights out of me." She said setting the well-polished guitar on the shelf.

"I just came in late to get my package when I heard this beautiful voice. That was you singing?"

"I told you yes, that was me singing. How many times do I have to tell you that?"

"I am amazed at your voice, why haven't we heard you sing in public?"

"I don't know, just shy, I have never had a reason or a desire to sing in front of anyone. Here in the back room I can do well, I can pour my heart out and most important of all I feel better after my little sessions."

"You have to sing that song for the celebration talent show."

"No, not me, I can't do that, absolutely not." She said closing the door and turning on the lights to the shop."

"Oh, yes, you will. I will help you, practice in front of me and that will help you overcome your shyness, but, allow the village to share in your gift."

"I'll think about it. May I help you with anything?'

"Yes, you can have dinner with me tomorrow night."

"Dinner? Where did that come from?"

"Well, it came from my mouth; let me show you…will you have dinner with me?" He said slowly holding his hands to his mouth for emphasis.

"You don't have to be sarcastic about it. Yes, I will have dinner with you." She said mocking him putting her hands to her mouth.

"I didn't realize until now that you are a very sarcastic person."

"If you are trying to get on my good side by giving me a compliment, I guess you are wasting your time." She managed to laugh.

"I'm sorry, I shouldn't have said that. I feel like I am on my left foot and the right one got stuck in my mouth." He laughed.

"I can see that picture you are funny. Maybe we can do better tomorrow night. What time tomorrow?"

"How about seven o'clock at your house, I'll pick you up, I mean." He stammered.

"That will be fine, I will be ready."

"Here is your package and will put it on your bill."

"Thank you Ivy, and am looking forward to tomorrow night." He said smiling.

"You are welcome and so am I." She said still stunned at the sudden appearance of Tully and his surprising appearance and invitation to dinner.

The brightly lit lamp posts seemed to echo in unison all through the small village 'we are on again, the war has ended and we can light the darkness once more, enjoy your lighted path.'

He could feel how relaxing it was remembered all the comments hot they had forgotten how pleasant it was to walk at night not having the heavy burden of fear of being a lit target for the enemy.

The next day both Ivy and Tully had mixed feelings about the impending dinner date.

They each decided to enjoy the evening and see what would transpire.

Tully and Ivy walked slowly to the small chip shop around the corner from where Ivy lived.

They both were hungry for fresh fish they used to enjoy before the fisherman went off to war and they had to close the shop for lack of food to sell as it was too dangerous to be on the Channel.

"Ivy, let's sit over here by the fireplace, you are shivering."

"I know, this is the end of May, but the evenings are still cool."

"It won't be long and summer will be here and the nights will be warmer."

"What are you doing for the celebration? I mean are you on a committee?"

"I am doing dog tricks with Sadie and Oscar."

"I didn't know you were an animal trainer as well as a vet."

"I just play around with them, just for fun. They are both very intelligent. It just gave me something to occupy my time."

"That is sad; I can picture you with the two dogs all alone…" She stopped before she said any more to make him feel bad about his loneliness.

"Don't feel sad about me, I have been so busy working and the Home Guards I haven't had time to be lonely. Are you referring to Jenny leaving me for another man?"

"No, I…I mean well, yes…I guess so. That must have been tragic for you."

"It was and a shock. But when she started drinking I knew things would either get worse or she would have to quit, I wasn't going to live with a lush." He said looking down at the red checkered table cloth and the flickering candle resting on it.

"Do you have any idea why she started drinking?"

"She always had sad moments while we were going together, then after we were married and found out she couldn't have children she cried a lot and I think drinking helped her live in denial. She wanted a large family. We both did. She shut me out more and more each day. Then that guy came into town wearing his uniform she evidently took to and that was that. She packed her bags and left me a note telling me good bye. No excuses just that she found someone she could talk to."

"How heart wrenching, I feel better about Darryl, he gave his life for our country but....sorry, I didn't mean to make you feel worse."

"That is all right, I finally have let her go and the pain like letting go of a beautiful balloon into the sky and watching it until it goes out of sight and can't see it any longer…that is how I did it."

"What a wonderful way to accept it, you are something else." She smiled at him realizing he was a very deep and thoughtful man.

"How did you overcome Darryl's death?"

"Singing my heart out and playing the guitar in the storage room." "You have singing and playing the guitar excellently and I have my two things, Sadie and Oscar." He laughed.

The couple talked and ate and laughed the rest of the evening sitting by the fireplace that gave them warmth along with thoughts of their prospective new relationship.

CHAPTER SEVENTEEN

"Annie, are you ready for our beauty night?" Cinny asked tapping on the bedroom door.

"I guess I am ready for this, I have dreaded tonight all day. I am not a frilly cosmetic person. "Anise admitted.

"I know, but it is time for us to catch up with the rest of the world. We can help each other apply it as well as we can. We will let each other know what looks natural and what doesn't."

"O.K. let's get this over with. Let me help you first and then me."

"We have to have some music first, let me find something that will get us in the mood." Cinny laughed at her reference to the Glen Miller music.

"That is a great idea, yes, this might not be so bad after all, and at least we can get our laugh in for the day."

They stood in front of the large wooden framed round mirror in Annie's bathroom dressed in their old ivory colored flannel pajamas and tapping their pink slippers as they rocked backed and forth and hummed to the music on the BBC, began the new experience with makeup.

"Now, Annie we have to cleanse our faces with this." Cinny said handing the cold cream jar to Anise as she began gently massaging the cream on her own face.

"What does this have to do with make up?"

"The shop girl said we have to have a very clean face before we apply the foundation." Cinny said rubbing the cream over her face. "Can't we just wash our face like we usually do with soap and water?"

"Oh, no, it has to be 'cleansed' with the companies face cream that goes with the makeup. Don't you see?"

"No, but I'll do what you want."

"Here is a clean cloth to clean off the cream and watch the dirt we take off that we weren't aware we had."

"Don't dab at your skin, gently wipe it off, like this." She said moving the cloth carefully over her face.

"I don't see any dirt, do you on yours?"

"Well not yet let me finish."

"You don't have any either. This is a waste of time and money."

"No, it is not, it just means our faces were clean because we hadn't worn make up today."

"Now what do we do?"

"Here is the moisture we need so we won't get wrinkles."

"What does that have to do with wearing make up?"

"Anise, please, if we get wrinkles our makeup won't look good … that is what…"

"I know, the counter girl said. All right pour some out in my hand so I won't get wrinkles."

"Not too much just a small amount so it won't be too thick because our faces would look like it was caked with goo."

"We are ready for the makeup. She said to do it over the face then with a circular motion rub it into the face."

The girls sat on the bedroom floor with their hair wrapped with a towel in turban style experiencing their first night in the makeup world.

"How does that look?" Cinny asked holding up the hand mirror.

"I can't tell it did anything, well, maybe your face looks smoother."

"See, what did I tell you?"

"What about mine, does my face look smother?"

"Let me see, let's go into the bathroom with the brighter light." Cinny said, dancing around.

"That isn't bad, I think your face is smoother, I really think it is, Annie."

"The real test will be when we wear it to work. Everyone we work with and the customers hopefully will let us know."

"You mean actually wear it out in public, in daylight, tomorrow?"

"Why not, I thought you were sincere about this, or were you just playing games?"

"No, I mean, I am serious, I just never thought about wearing it to work, only evenings, after dark."

"That is better, we can try it after dark and it won't be as noticeable as in daylight." Anise said taking the cleansing cream jar lid off.

"We are not finished, don't take it off yet. We still have the eyebrow pencil and mascara and lipstick to apply."

"What eyebrow pencil and what is mascara?"

"Annie, don't you know anything?"

"No, I don't, show me what you are talking about. You put it on me and then I can do yours if you want.

Now, be still Cinny stop dancing around you will smear it all over."

Cinny sat on the floor holding Anise's chin in her hand to keep them both still while she made light feathery strokes with the brow pencil. Then applying the last touches of mascara she stood up helping her sister to check the end results.

They looked into the bathroom mirror comparing the full made up face of Anise to the partial one of Cinny. "Well, what do you think?"

"I am not sure, what do you think?"

"I think you look beautiful, now let me put your lipstick on to see for sure."

"Oh, Annie, you look beautiful, don't you like it?"

"Not bad, is it?"

"Not bad, it is outstanding, wait until little Matt sees this." Cinny said dancing around her.

"Now don't get carried away I don't look that different."

"You can say what you want but it makes you look glamorous and stylish. Now we have to do this when we go for dinner tomorrow night with the guys. Right?"

"Yes, but you have to do it for me, I don't think I can right now.'"

"I will only be glad to, now I have to finish mine."

The two sisters chatted and laughed about their new look and decided what dress to wear the following night and the style they wanted for their hair.

The music flowed and they moved to the music checking each other out in the full length mirror discovering themselves in a new light and mood.

The following morning Cinny went into the Jarvis Chemist Shop to buy some more cloths to remove the makeup they would be using more and more.

"Hello, Ivy, how are you today?"

"I am doing well, how are you and what can I do to help you?"

"I need some more cloths to remove make up that Annie and I are starting to wear. Do you wear it at all?" "No, I just wash my face." She smiled.

"Have you ever thought about wearing it?"

"Well there was a salesman one day tried to convince me to, but I didn't want to be bothered."

"Annie and I are going to wear it tonight when we go with Matt and Collin to dinner."

"Where are you going to dinner?"

"The Beach Front Café."

"I am going to be there and will see how you both look and then I will let you know what I think. Is that all right?"

"Yes, who are you going with?"

"Well…Tully asked me out."

"Really? That is marvelous. Yes, we will be sure you see us and then if you like it come over and we will help you know how to put it on."

"Don't let anyone know what we are doing, please keep it to yourself, I am not comfortable letting anyone know I am even interested until I decide quietly, ok?"

"Yes, you are like Annie she is a very discreet person too. I think you and Tully would make a good pair, I never thought about it before, but I think that is great."

"Now, Cinny don't get carried away, it is only a dinner."

"All right, I promise, put the cloths on my bill, ok?"

"Yes, will do and I will see you tonight." She winked at her leaving the shop with her sack of cloths for her new adventure into the world of glamour.

Running through the Tea Shop to the kitchen Cinny grabbed Anise by the arm taking her outside to where the patio tables had just been set for the lunch customers

"What are you doing, Cinny?"

"Shhhh, Annie, I have something to tell you. Sit down for a minute. I just saw Ivy and she has a date with guess who?"

"How should I know?"

"Tully asked her out to dinner at the Beach Front Café, where we will be tonight, isn't that a coincidence?"

"Well, I suppose, it is a surprise they are having dinner, I must say that is wonderful. I have always liked her, she is five years older than me and I have thought that she and I would end up being old maids after Darryl died. This is nice. I can actually see them together."

"Me too, now the real secret is when she sees us tonight she wants to look at our makeup to see if she wants to try it too. But we have to be very nonchalant and let anyone know we want to show her how we look."

"That is funny. I can see us now; we will parade ourselves around the café and make a right fool of ourselves."

"Now, don't be so silly, we will just make sure she sees us up close. I thought when we see them we could go over to their table and ask her if she is on a committee for the celebration and if not we could use some help with the food. How does that sound for a casual meeting?"

"You are very good at this little sister, when did you get so creative?"

"Oh, I don't know, I have watched you and guess it rubbed off on me." Cinny said running back inside.

The setting sun brought a golden radiance through the large bay windows that gave warmth to the wooden furniture covered with aqua blue patterned cushions to the café'.

"This is a beautiful; I love this time of day, don't you?" Cinny asked looking around for Ivy.

"Yes, mine too; we are fortunate to live here, where it is so clean. Our beaches are clean and our village is outstandingly clean. After some of the places we were in on the Continent home is paradise." Matt said.

"I know what you mean, I don't know if it was just the war or if those places were always that way," Collin said.

"I suppose you both have many things you want to forget about the war." Anise said.

"I don't have any bad experiences up close; I just had my friends die in their planes as they crashed. I am grateful I didn't have anything that gave me nightmares like some of the guys in my squad did. It was bad enough just losing friends." Matt said.

"I didn't either, we are lucky, some of the guys had nightmares so bad they would scream and wake us all up and then we couldn't get back to sleep thinking we would either be next in their dreams or that we would have to watch closely someone dying and being shot up." Collin said.

"Oh, Annie, look, Ivy and Tully, over there, fancy that, have you ever seen them together before?"

"No, this is something new. But now that I have seen them, they look like they go together." Matt said smiling at the new couple. "Now, don't go thinking this is serious, it is just a dinner, not a wedding." Anise said.

"Annie, I need to freshen up, go with me?"

"Sure, we will be back soon."

"We won't go away, we promise." Matt said winking at her.

The two young women slowly maneuvered over to the table where Ivy and Tully were in deep conversation.

"Sorry to interrupt, Ivy we are going to freshen up, would you like to go with us?" Cinny asked.

"Well, yes, I suppose so. I'll be back in a minute Tully."

"Take your time, we have already ordered so will say' hi' to the guys while you freshen up." He said standing up and pulling out the chair for Ivy noticing the sweet perfume she was wearing.

"Were we too obvious, Ivy?" Cinny asked softly.

"No, it went very smoothly."

"You both look wonderful. You look the same only…well…your faces look smoother and your eyes larger and I love your lipstick. I even like the mascara, it isn't too thick. You applied it very well, it looks natural. You will have to come over and help me, will you?"

"Of course we will, let us know and we will get together. It will be fun. Mood music is the key."

"Mood music, what is that all about?"

"Oh, just our way of relaxing and having some fun.'

"Please don't let anyone know I am coming over for this promise?" Ivy pleaded/

"We promise, not a soul." Cinny winked.

"We better get back see you later Ivy." Annie said escorting her back to the table.

"Annie, care to dance? "Matt asked before she could sit down.

"Sure, but, I am not very good, I have not danced very much."

Matt led her onto the small dance floor and took her into his arms.

"How was it here at home during the war, were you ever frightened?"

"I wasn't until … well; mum and dad were killed in the Blitz. Then everything frightened us. Cinny and I were uneasy all the time expecting to be bombed every day. Then one Sunday the vicar gave such a good sermon about how good people go to heaven that we decided we were good people and if we should die we would go there and be with our parents. I suppose that was the good part of our parent's death and our wonderful memories of them."

"That is wonderful. You both are good girls and have nothing to worry about… except me keeping my hands off you." He laughed.

"You are just being silly now 'Mattie'." "Don't you ever call me that again, or…"

"Or what?" She laughed at him.

"This." He stopped dancing held her tightly so she couldn't move and gave her the biggest kiss she ever had.

"Do you mind?" She said catching her breath and straightening her dress.

"No, I don't mind at all. Call me 'Mattie' again and I promise this will happen every time you do.

So keep in mind what I just said and did." He laughed.

"You really think you are funny, but you…"

"What?"

"You are not funny that's all."

"Let's get back to the table and eat, all of a sudden I am starved." He said leading her back to the grinning onlookers at their table.

Anise made a mental note never to call him Mattie again….unless… he would kiss her.

CHAPTER EIGHTEEN

The Ladies Auxiliary broke off into the committees for the celebration reports of their progress to the heads of the committee for each assignment and to resolve any issue that might have developed since the last meeting.

"Hazel, we need someone to make sure the children are where they need to be to sit on the ice cream makers as the ones in charge churn it until harden." Irene said.

"What about Marilee and Wesley? Would they be able to take charge of it? We need at least ten children to take turns and not get tired.

"I think they can handle that, Marilee can be trusted to follow through and keep everything going properly. Her father and I depend on her and Wesley every day for something, so I will ask them and let you know." Irene said proud of her capable children.

"How is Les doing after his fall?" Missy asked as she made notes in her book.

"He and Nigel are doing very well, you know Nigel wants to start giving music lessons, do you know of anyone that would like to take from him?"

"I don't but will ask around and see if I can find someone willing to start. It might take some time before we can truly trust him. We need someone very strong and willing to be with him."

"I think I will ask Wesley if he will, we have talked about him taking some kind of music. I will let you know." Irene said.

"Anise, I wanted to tell you how attractive you and Cinny have been looking lately. What have you been doing to yourselves?" Missy asked.

"Well, Cinny had this idea about the new makeup they have been advertising and we tried some and liked it. If you are interested let her know and she will help you get started." Anise said making notes about food orders.

"I don't know about that, for me any way."

"Well, suit yourself."

"Did you hear about Ivy having dinner with Tully?"

"What was that?" Lucy Burkhart asked.

"Yes, Tully Shepard and Ivy." Missy whispered.

"You don't have to whisper, I will tell you what you would like to know." Ivy said smiling.

"Sorry, I didn't know you were here tonight." Missy mumbled.

"That is all right, we only had dinner that was last week that is all. What would you like to know about it?"

"Well nothing, I thought was very nice for you both. I can see you together." Missy smiled.

"How are you and Collin doing Cinny?" Irene asked.

"We are just friends, just like Annie and Matt."

"I think it is wonderful how everyone is going together. We need more families here in the village. Hope we have many weddings to look forward to in the future." Irene said.

The village hall filled with chatter about all the new relationships that were forming.

With the issues coming up concerning each committee there was plenty to talk about that evening.

CHAPTER NINETEEN

"Matt, are you busy tonight?" Collin asked.

"No, what do you need?"

"I'll meet you at your shop at five; I have something I need to talk to you about."

"You sound mysterious. Sure, I'll be here. Jeremy will close tonight; maybe we could grab a bite?"

"That would be great, see you then."

Matt continued making his list of things he needed for the decorations for the celebration.

His idea for the huge golden paper moon and indigo color cardboard sea was his special project and had made arrangements with the village swing band to play "Paper Moon" in the beginning of the evening and then later when her was going to ask Anise to marry him. He had that planned since he was in France how he was going to ask her. The celebration gave him the perfect opportunity and that was the reason he wanted to be in charge of decorations to make sure the moon and sea would be perfectly situated above the dance floor.

He knew Hazel had been surprised when he phoned her asking her to be the head of the committee.

His father was still in Cornwall and he needed to let him know he needed some time to go to France and start his apprenticeship with his old friend, Antoine Cobre'.

Jeremy had agreed to take over for him while he was gone and would hire his friend to rotate their schedules and asked for permission to have Wesley Gates to help out on Saturdays.

He would be leaving for France the next day after the celebration for France and hoped Anise would promise to marry him after he got situated there with a place to live for them to start out in the first year of their new life together.

His concern about her leaving the village was Cinny and the well-established family business. It was more than a business, it had been their life. A year would be a long time to be away from her sister.

"Collin, just a minute until Jeremy finishes his errand for me, he will be back in a few minutes."

"I just needed to talk to you about asking Cinny to marry me. I have to make a plan and need you to help me. There are so many obstacles to overcome. I am sure you will too when you make your plans for you and Anise."

"I was just thinking about that, and it is going to take some deep thought and many ideas."

"Hi Jeremy, thank you for not taking your time, Collin and I have some business to discuss and will be at the Beach Front Café' if you need me. Will you close for me tonight?"

"Yes, of course I wanted to organize some of the new items you brought back from London. Did you have any specific instructions about them?"

"No, I trust your judgment. See you tomorrow you don't have to come in until noon if you want."

"Thank you I could use some free time. See you at noon."

The Café' was filled with customers enjoying the setting sun that radiated its usual golden glow giving the atmosphere added attraction to the wood and blue fabric decor.

The two friends stared out the large bay window by their favorite table.

"So, Collin, how can I help you with your plans? You are still planning on going to medical school?"

"Yes, I am more determined than ever. I talked to Dr. Burkhart the other day and he said he will help me enroll. I need to get my papers from my former university for the pharmacist degree I attended and he will go with me.

Now, I don't know what to do about Cinny, I want to ask her to marry me and I don't know how school will go and how we will live or where because of her business. I need your help sorting this all out. I have to make it work and I don't want to live separately from her all the years I need to go to university."

"I know, I am having the same problems, I need to finish my apprenticeship and I don't want to be away from Anise and what to do about her business. I think the first thing we need to do it decide what could be done about the business so we could have them be with us. That seems to be our largest obstacle, don't you think?"

"Yes, you know, when we were in London I wondered if their Uncle
Reggie might like to take over for them, does he have children?"

"He has a son, I think but I can't remember much about him."

"Will you find out more about him and let's take a quick trip to see Uncle Reggie and see what we could come up with, there might be someone else in the family that would like to take over the business and keep it in the family. Isn't Reggie their father's brother? Is there another brother or sister?'

"I don't know about other family members, we will ask him. Let's get our work schedules taken care of leave day after tomorrow if we can."

"That will work for me; Ivy is always willing to get rid of me. She is attached to the shop and I am sure she will love to take over for me when I want to leave and go to school."

"You are fortunate, I have to get father back here and tell him what I am doing and get him to help me or sell the shop. I am not working in the shop the rest of my life."

"I think we can get things in order, even though it may take some maneuvering."

"The more I think about Uncle Reggie the more I like that idea. He isn't that old. I think he is at least ten years younger than the girl's father. He could still paint, and remember he told them he would think about moving here when they asked him when we were there?'

"I forgot about that he did sound interested. I can't wait to get there and find out more."

"Let's eat; all of a sudden I am starved." Matt said reaching for the menu.

CHAPTER TWENTY

"Ivy, how are you today?" Anise asked from behind the bakery counter.

"I am doing very well, thank you. I was wondering if I could come over to your house some night and play around with the makeup you and Cinny have been using. If you would tell me what you are using I could order mine from the salesman. It would only take a day or two to receive it from them."

"Sure let me get her she is in the kitchen. Cinny please come out front Ivy wants to talk to you."

"Hello Ivy how are you today?"

"I am doing very well. I was asking Annie what make up you are using so I can order me some and then you can help me learn how to use it. Would you mind?"

"That would be fun, let me write it down and then you won't forget. We could have a girl's night with food from our shop. Let us know when you get your order, and then we can plan what night."

"Thank you both you have been so nice to me. I appreciate any help at my age."

"I know, I feel the same way. But guess we are lucky not to be any older, appreciate what we have and make the best of it."

"That is a very good attitude. I agree I am grateful for what I have."

"Have you been seeing Tully lately?"

"Yes, we went to dinner last night as a matter of fact."

"That is so nice for you; do you think it is serious?'

"I don't know, maybe. Only time will tell."

"I know what you mean time will tell." Annie said.

They relaxed outside on the patio and had tea and biscuits and chatted about their similar experiences with the dates they were having with the guys that they had recently started to date.

"Lucy, hello, come join us would you like some tea?'

"Thank you, yes, I would, thank you."

Anise hurried into the shop and brought out a large steaming pot of tea for them to share.

"Cinny, I was wondering if you are still dating Collin Jarvis.'

"Well, I don't know if you would say dating exactly, we go to dinner and a movie once in a while. Why?'

"My husband just told me he is planning to go to medical school; do you know anything about that?"

"No, he hasn't said a word about it. That is a surprise, where and when will he go/'

"I don't know the details but sounds like he is getting his papers from his degree as pharmacist together so it must be soon."

"I'll have to ask him about it."

"I am so happy to see you young couples forming friendships and hope they are serious ones, we need more families in the village we have too many singles." She said.

"These things can't be rushed Lucy, it takes time enough to get acquainted."

"Time, you girls have known these boys all your lives. But I do understand how you must feel."

"Yes, so let's talk about something else." Anise asked.

"How is Les and Nigel coming along with their drinking?"

"Hazel said they are doing very well, in fact they haven't had a drink since the day Les flew down the hill on his ladder."

"That is wonderful. You know, who likes him?"

"No, who?" Cinny asked.

"Daphne Shaw, that's who, she told Missy she has liked him for years but because he drank she would never consider going with him."

"That is incredible, I would have never thought for one moment about them. Have they gone out yet?"

"No, but Missy said she was going to let Hazel know so she could pass it on to Les."

"When I hear something I will let you girls know. I must be getting home to make dinner."

"Good to see you Lucy, keep in touch."

"I don't feel so odd now that I heard that about Daphne. It just lets us know we are all alike inside, wanting someone to be with." Ivy sighed wistfully.

"We are all alike. We don't want to be alone for the rest of our lives. We all need someone to share our life with don't us? Anise said.

"Yes, you both are right. We need men." Cinny said jumping up before Annie could stop her from saying anything else.

"Sorry Ivy, she is my little sister and I have no control over her mouth."

"That's all right, I thought she was funny. We all need to laugh and stop being so serious don't we?"

"Yes, Cinny and I promised each other we would share a laugh every day and we have kept that promise, we have a very funny village.

"We do, and a kind and caring one as well."

The Brooker sisters hummed as they cleaned the Tea Shop and Bakery after the busy day.

Anise turned on the radio and listened to the popular music.

"I love music; it makes me feel so good. I can be kind of low and then I hear a wonderful song and it brightens my day. Speaking of music did you hear about Ivy playing the guitar at the talent show for the celebration?"

"Yes, she is quite talented. I heard her play one day she wasn't aware I was in the shop late one night when he father waited on me for an order that came in. She was in the storage room and didn't think anyone was around."

"That is good for her; she must have many sad songs after losing Daryl. I never knew what to say to her about it so I never did just the sympathy card and flowers for the memorial services."

"I know me too. I did the same thing, I always feel so awkward at times like those."

"What do you think about Collin going to medical school?"

"I was shocked to hear it, he has never said one word about it, and I wonder why he never brought it up?'

"Maybe he wanted to wait until he was sure it would happen. Those things take time."

"I will ask him when we have dinner tomorrow night."

"Well, are you ready to go home?'

"Yes, we have such a long way to go." She laughed.

They unlocked the cottage door and turned on the lamps. Let's have some tea and relax before we turn in." Anise said.

"Sounds good to me, I keep thinking about Collin going to medical school. I can't wait to ask him about it."

"I would like to talk to you about that. What would you do if he asked you to marry him and leave the village to live with him where ever he goes to school?"

"That is incredible; I was just thinking that very thought. With our shops what could I do?"

"Go with him."

"What about you and the business?"

"I would manage very well with the young ones that have decided to stay here, Polly, and some others have told me they want to stay and not go back home. There is nothing for them any longer after the bombings of their families and homes. There is nothing to go back to." Anise said.

"Isn't that sad?"

"It is, but you know nothing lasts forever and they have good attitudes and will get on with their lives. So many of them are staying here including the ones at the Applegate farm and others."

"I just wanted to let you know when you talk to Collin tomorrow night and if he should ask you to marry him, that you are free to go with him and I will make do, I am not worried. As much as I should miss you things will be fine."

"Oh, Annie, I can hardly think about not living with you or close to you and see you every day, what would I do without you?"

"I know, me too you, but remember you have to live your life, have children, make memories for them the way we have them with our mum and dad, that is what life is all about, families."

"What makes you think I would say yes if he asked?"

"Please, Cinny, this is me you are talking to, I've seen you with him, you remind me of the cartoon character in love with the other one and its heart shows though its clothes beating like a drum."

"Be serious, I am not that obvious."

"Oh, yes you are my little muffin."

"Oh, no, why didn't you tell me. I must have embarrassed myself many times and didn't know it. I wonder if Collin noticed."

"I think it would be safe to say he has. But you were very sweet about it, not annoying or aggressive, just adorable."

"Adorable, that's a fine thing to say about a grown woman."

"Well, almost grown." Annie said smiling approvingly at her little sister.

CHAPTER TWENTY ONE

The town hall was filled with each committee chairman and their assistants as Hazel brought them to order.

"Thank you everyone for your attendance tonight. We need to have you report your committee's progress and if you need help please don't hesitate to ask.

We don't want anything to go wrong for this will be a splendid night for us all and we want to work out any issues beforehand.

If you don't have any questions I would like each committee chairman to vocally give me a report on how things are coming along.

Are there any questions?"

"Yes, I needed to get your permission to ask Reggie Brooker to help me with the decorations. I think I bit off a little more than I can handle alone, he is the uncle of Anise and Cinny Brooker and lives in London and is an artist."

"Well of course if he wants to help that would be wonderful, have you asked him?"

"Yes, I have and he said he would be happy to help out. He will be here this weekend."

"Thank you Matt for letting me know about this, I appreciate your interest in making our night special. I will talk more with you later."

"Annie, did you know about this?"

"No, I had no idea I wonder why Uncle Reggie didn't let us know he was coming."

"Ask Matt, he will know."

"That Matt, he should have told us before this meeting instead of announcing it to the whole meeting."

"Now, Annie, calm down don't get your feathers ruffled, he didn't mean anything by it, he is a typical man, in his own little world and doesn't intend to offend."

"I suppose you are right, I should at least let him explain before I tell him off."

Each chairman reported their progress and problems and when the last one sat down it was time for refreshments.

"I want to thank Anise and Cinny for bringing their wonderful bakery cakes and biscuits and tea tonight, we always enjoy them so much and are a real treat. Please Annie will you bless the food?"

The simple blessing on the food brought tears to the eyes of everyone there that evening repeating in their hearts the gratitude to God that the war was finally over and they all had survived.

The food was set in the middle of the table and the line began to form to fill their plates.

Settling down to eat, Irene sat down and several of the women joined her.

"Irene, we needed to ask you about Marilee. Is she all right?"

"What do you mean is she all right?"

"Well, I was talking to her and the Murphy boys the other day and all of a sudden she just ran off coughing." Missy said.

"Me too, I was asking her about how her little group of children were doing with the schedule of taking turns to sit on the buckets of ice cream. She and the boys were walking down the street with Wesley and were telling her about something they were doing for the celebration and she cleared her throat and coughed something and left suddenly." Hazel said.

"Oh, don't worry, she just has some allergies. She has been coughing and sneezing quite a bit lately." Irene smiled knowing Marilee was doing her best to stop making fun of the boys as she had warned her even when she wasn't around her mother.

"Annie, I wanted to let you know I am sorry I didn't let you know sooner before this meeting about Reggie, but I have been out of town and didn't have the chance, forgive me?"

Matt asked putting his arm around her waist.

"I will, but tell me about his visit, we need to make up a room for him. Did you say he would be here this weekend?"
"Yes, he and your Aunt Lily, she is coming as well."

"Auntie Lily?'

"Yes, she said she hasn't seen you girls for such a long time she wanted to come with Reggie. So make her a room up as well."

"I am glad we finally found out about this family gathering, everyone knew but the family." Annie said getting upset.

"Now, please, this just accelerated so quickly I didn't have the chance to fore warn you until tonight. I only intended to ask for his help with the decorations." Matt said reaching for her hand to draw her near to console her.

"This is such a surprise but a good one, we will freshen everything up tomorrow for them and make them feel at home." Cinny said.

"Yes, and put fresh flowers in the rooms open the windows and bring in some light.

Those rooms have been shut up for years glad we have some time before they come. This will be quite enjoyable to have company. It has been years since anyone has come for a visit." Annie sighed. "Annie, I am so relieved you are taking this so well, I only wanted to get Reggie's help with the art work I wanted to do to make everything as real as possible. I have had this idea for a long time and this celebration was the perfect time to make it happen. I will tell you more someday when we have the time and privacy." Matt winked at Annie and made her blush.

"How about tomorrow night you and Collin come to dinner at seven?"

"We will be there, may we bring something?"

"No, you don't have to bring anything, just yourselves and Annie winked back at him and this time he blushed.

They gathered their empty refreshment cartons, tea pots, and dinner ware together with the help of Collin and Matt.

The foursome carried the cartons to Matt's old blue pickup he bought before the war.

"Thank you for your help, we appreciate not having to phone Gus for a ride back home, he usually goes to bed early." Cinny said.

"You are so welcome, whenever you need a ride let us know, your little car can't hold much."

"I know, we really need to get a pick up don't we?"

"Yes, you do, well; I guess not, Gus doesn't mind does he?"

"No, he doesn't that is part of his job, we only need to plan ahead with him as I said he goes to bed early."

"Let's go gang; we need to get our girls home for their beauty sleep." Matt chuckled.

CHAPTER TWENTY TWO

The slight rustle of the leaves behind Ron and Olive caught their attention. Turning to look back to see what was making the faint noise they noticed the movement of the flowers and foliage behind the park bench they were sitting on that evening.

"Ron, that bush is moving, look." She said not wanting to yell.

"Oh, Olive, please, don't be so..." Ron stopped to look again at the movement.

"Look it is moving." Olive said running down the sidewalk away from the moving shrub.

"Wait, Olive, stay with me, I don't want you to go without me, I don't want you to be alone." He said holding his shaking wife.

Then they watched as Nigel fell out of the large bush he had been hiding in doing his usual camouflage routine with leaves and flowers stuck all over him.

"Nigel, what are you doing at this time of night?"

"Just... Uh...pro...tec..ting our vil...l age from Hit...ler and his devils." He slurred.

"Are you all right?" Ron asked untangling him from the branch that caught his fall.

"You can't do this; remember we told you if you don't stop this we will report you to the police?"

"I know, but..."

"This is the last time you will do this Nigel, come with us, we are taking you to the station, next time you will hurt yourself or someone else."

"No, no…I can go on my own. I will meet you there."

"We will walk behind you all the way, so don't think we are letting you go, we have had enough of this."

"I thought you and Les quit drinking?"

"He did, but I never said I would for sure."

"You will get hurt one day if you don't stop it now, we are all concerned about you."

The small police station was quiet as the trio walked inside together.

Ron escorted Nigel up to the counter ringing the silver bell to get someone's attention.

"Yes, how may I help you?" The tall policeman dressed in the usual dark navy uniform said looking at Nigel's appearance with a smile.

"This man will not stop hiding in the bushes in the park and scare everyone that goes there. Last time he frightened children and they still have nightmares from him jumping out at them." Ron said still holding Nigel so he wouldn't be able to get away.

"We are well acquainted aren't we Nigel?"

"Yes, how are you Marvin?"

"I am doing very well, thank you. Remember the last time you were in here we told you we would arrest you and put you in jail?"

"Yes, but we are not safe, the Japanese are still fighting us in the jungles. Don't you know that?"

"Yes, we do, and the key words are fighting in the jungles, not here or the continent. What are we going to do with you Nigel?"

"I don't know, I'm tired, I need to go home to bed, Ron will take me home, won't you Ron?"

"I suppose so, what do you think officer?"

"All right then, but you must come back tomorrow and we will have to sort things out, you must promise Nigel that you will come back tomorrow before noon."

"I will bring him here before noon, thank you for being so kind. See you then." Ron said leading Nigel outside with him on one side and Olive on the other.

Ron and Olive walked Nigel home and unlocked the small cottage door for him where he and his younger brother and wife lived.

"Is he all right?" They asked.

"Yes, I will be here in the morning around ten o'clock, so be sure he is here when I return." Ron said walking slowly out the door.

"Yes, he will be here."

"What happened now?"

"I was just patrolling our village and they saw me and took me to the police station. I am tired, I am going to bed."

The morning sun warmed Nigel's face as its rays woke him to the morning he would have to face the charges made the night before.

"Nigel, do you want breakfast?" His sister-in-law asked as she stood outside his bedroom door.

"No, thank you, I have a headache, just some tea. Thank you."

He showered and shaved moving slowly not wanting to face the day. All he could remember was promising someone something that he didn't want to do.

"Nigel, Ron is here to take you to the station. I hope you will get help and stop this juvenile business of hiding in the bushes." His brother said.

"Tell him I am coming just as soon as I finish getting dressed." He said.

"Nigel, Les is on the phone, do you have time to say hello?"

"No, tell him I'll phone him later."

Ron and Nigel walked leisurely and silently to the police station, as they walked up the steps Nigel stopped and asked. "Ron, please don't say anything about this to anyone, will you please?'

"I won't and Olive won't either, we have already discussed it this morning. We had an idea about helping you."

"What would that be?" He asked stopping at the top of the steps.

"We wondered if you would like to come stay with us for a while and work with us in the store, we could use the help and it would give you something to do and focus on while you are trying to get your life together."

"Me, work with you and Olive in your store?"

"Yes, in our store. Wait on customers, help me stock shelves, unpack boxes and clean the shop."

"That sounds like a lot of work."

"It will be, but you will be so tired at night you will not want to go out and drink, that would be the purpose of it all."

"Can I think about it for a while?"

"Yes, but remember you need something to get you out of your bad habit, something to break the routine. We would be there to talk to and help you when you needed someone to talk to. You and your brother don't get along and his wife either."

"They just put up with me that is for certain. They could use a break I suppose."

"Let's see what they say here."

The two men went inside looking around once again for someone to come to the counter.

"Hello, may I help you" The younger policeman asked.

"Is Marvin here?"

"No, not yet, but he will any minute now, you may wait for him if you want."

"Yes, we will wait for him." Nigel said softly going over to sit on the bench.

"Nigel, good, you are here, please you and Ron come back into my office and we will talk about last night."

"How are you feeling this morning?"

"I have a headache."

"I would imagine you would, and be grateful that is all. You could have had a serious fall. We have to find a way to help you; we decided not to have you put in jail that would not help you stop drinking."

"We may have a solution." Ron said.

"What would that be?"

"Nigel, you tell him what we were just talking about."

Nigel explained what Ron and Olive had thought might help him.

"This means you have to promise in writing, that you will do this, I think it is a wonderful idea. You would be helping them as well as they would be helping you. This is what I call a win, win, solution. I like it and I really think it will work. Do you think you can make a promise and not wangle out of it?"

"I think I can do it, I am willing to try it. I don't want to go to jail." "Good for you, let me get the form and have you sign it. I hope I never have to see you here again unless it is to come here after you have fulfilled the sentence and we can tear up the form."

"I think I can do this."

Nigel signed the papers promising to work and live with Ron and Olive every day for two months without one drink of alcohol and not one day or night of hiding in the bushes.

CHAPTER TWENTY THREE

"Uncle Reggie, Aunt Lily, we are so happy you are here. It has been so long since we have seen you Aunt Lily. How are you?"

"I am doing very well, now especially since the war is over. London is so quiet now we hardly know what to do."

"Well, there is much to do as far as clean up and rebuilding is concerned." Reggie said taking the cases upstairs to the freshly cleaned rooms.

"Girls, this is so nice and so clean and bright."

"Yes, we hope the cleaning fumes won't bother you, are you going to be all right?"

"Of course, we will keep the windows open; you have lovely lace curtains for help keeping the insects out."

"Mummy always used this pattern she said it was the best for that." Cinny said.

"I am so sorry for your loss. I can't imagine how much you miss them. How did you manage?" Lily asked.

"It wasn't easy, but we were so busy we didn't have much time to feel sorry for ourselves. We would crash at night and couldn't stay awake long enough to cry. We see now it was a blessing."

"Isn't that true, some of our hardest trials have the most normal solutions."

"How long have you been back from France, Aunt Lily?"

"Only about a week, it took some time to arrange things to move back home. I am glad I am here, I missed London. It was a very interesting challenge though taking design classes in French. I sat in ignorance for the first few months then finally the language started to make sense. I was lonely but made some good friends."

"We will let you unpack and would you like a shower before dinner?"

"Yes, that would be nice, what time is it?"

"About seven, is that all right with you both?"

"Yes, they nodded."

The wonderful aroma from the kitchen floated into the candle lit dining room.

"Please sit down and we will bring the rest of the meal in. Hope you are hungry we have made enough for an army."

"Are we the only ones dinning?" Reggie asked.

"Yes, why?"

"I needed to ask Matt some questions about his decoration ideas. Would it be all right if we held dinner until he could come and maybe Collin as well?"

"Sure, Cinny will you phone them both for me and I will put the meal back in the oven to stay warm."

"Hope this isn't too much trouble." Reggie said.

"No, in fact that is a good idea; Cinny needs to ask Collin some questions about his plans for the future." Anise smiled.

"They will be here shortly." Cinny said helping Annie with the plates.

"We should have invited them, I never thought about it until he said something about them."

"Yes, I can't wait until I find out what is going on with him." Cinny said.

"That was quick, come on in to the dining room. We will bring the meal."

"Good to see you boys, how was your trip home?"

"Very smooth, we appreciate your help with the celebration. You have questions?"

"Yes, I need to see where you want everything and estimate the sizes." Reggie winked.

"What kind of decorations are you going to have?"

Annie asked.

"It is a secret, we want to surprise everyone. With your uncle's talent it will be awesome." Matt said.

"By the way, we heard some interesting news last night at the meeting in the town hall about you Collin."

"Oh, what was that?"

"That you are going to medical school?"

"What?"

"You heard me; Lucy Burkhart told us you were putting in your papers with the Doctor's help to a university."

"I had no idea anyone else knew, sorry I wanted to tell you myself. Yes, I am going to medical school. I will tell you later, later after dinner?"

"Sure we can go for a walk."

The light chatter of plans for the future and the celebration filled the dining room until it was time to clear the table.

"Cinny, you and Collin go for a walk; Matt will help me with the dishes. O.K.?" Anise said.

"Sure, let me get my sweater. Come on, Collin, I can't wait to hear about your plans." Cinny said taking him by the hand.

"Anise, I think Reggie and I will leave you and Matt and go to bed, we are tired. Do you mind?"

"Of course, please, I am sure you are tired. See you in the morning."

"Good night."

"Well, Ma….Matt, it is just you and me kid."

"Yes, it is and you almost got a kiss didn't you?" Matt laughed.

"Almost, but I caught…"

Before she could finish he took her arm and brought her to him and gave her a kiss ignoring his promise.

"I didn't call you Mattie, and you kissed me anyway, how can I win?"

"You can't. Will you marry me?" Matt blurted out.

"What did you say?"

"I didn't say anything, but I asked you if you will marry me?"

"What brought that on?"

"Brought that on?"

"Can't you hear?"

"Can't you talk?"

"Let's start over, I asked you if you will marry me?"

"I am too old for you." Anise said scrubbing the dishes.

"There is not one person that would see us together and ever think I was younger than you."

"Maybe not today, but there would come a time in a few years that it would start to show."

"I promise I will take such good care of you that will not happen." He took the dish out of her hands and turned her around to look into her bright blue eyes and brushed a sun streaked curl from her eye.

"Don't look at me like that." She said trying to pull away.

"I will, and I will look at you like this forever." He said holding on to her.

"I can't believe how stubborn you are Matthew Rutledge."

"I can't believe how stubborn you are Anise Brooker."

"You sound like an echo."

"Are you going to answer my question?"

"I have to think about it, you caught me totally off guard."

"When will you give me the answer?"

"I don't know, is there a time limit on it?"

"No, but I don't want you to take forever to give me the answer… yes."

"As soon as I feel the correct answer I will let you know, you will be the first one I will tell. Is that all right?"

"As long as you promise I am the first one to know."

"I promise, you will be the first one to know."

As Collin and Cinny walked arm in arm on the cool sand the moonlight danced across the English Channel as though it found something to be happy about.

The stars seemed brighter and the sky velvet as they slowly continued their walk while Collin told Cinny about his plans for the future and the part he wanted her to play.

When he finished by asking her to marry him she suddenly jumped up into his arms giving him the answer he dreamed she would say making it a perfect night to remember and more fulfilling than Matt's had been.

CHAPTER TWENTY FOUR

The gray cast sky matched Les' mood. He arose that morning needing a drink and could hardly control his urge to run to the pub and buy a bottle of something, anything at that point.

He continued to dress for the day and try to push through the overwhelming desire to drink.

Unlocking the shop he made the decision he would take everything off the shelves and sort through each piece of clothing and check to see what sizes he needed to order and while the folded garments were moved to the counter he would dust and polish the well-worn wooden shelves his father had built so many years ago.

Happy with his decision he heard the bell from the door opening and saw Hazel come in and at that moment felt she knew he needed her this morning for it was her first visit in a week.

"Hazel, how good to see you, how did you know I was struggling this morning more than usual?"

"I don't know, I just knew it was time I brought you a basket and pick up the last one I left."

"I'll get it for you; the basket has been my life line lately. Did you hear about Nigel hiding in the bushes the other night and scaring Olive and Ron?"

"Yes, I did and he is staying with them now for a while. That is good for them all, Ron needs someone to watch over and keep himself busy and stop his flirtatious behavior." She said picking up the empty basket.

"Olive is a very attractive woman and a nice one; I never could understand why he would ever flirt with anyone else. I guess I never got the hang of romance. As you can see, I failed in my few attempts through the years."

"Who were you interested in?"

"You don't know them, it was during the war and I can't even remember their names."

"I know someone that has a crush on you."

"You what?"

"I know of someone that likes you."

"Now who could that be?" He said not taking her seriously.

"Daphne Shaw."

"Really?"

"Yes, really, she told us all at a committee meeting she always liked you and thought you were so handsome and at one time even had a crush on you."

"The point of that statement 'used to have a crush'.

"You are not listening to me Les, she thinks you are handsome. I think you should ask her out to dinner. Today, I will stay here until you phone her."

"You are intruding now Hazel and I don't know if I have the energy to have a relationship at my age."

"Please, if you can fly down the hill on that ladder and land on our lawn and not get hundreds of broken bones I think you are up to a simple relationship with Daphne. She is not that young you know, she looks good but she is up there in age too."

"You have a very forward sarcastic nature Hazel Grovenor." He smiled.

"Well, do you phone her or do I stay here all day?"

"Oh, all right, I'll call, but if she says no, that is it I will never listen to you again about this."

Hazel stood beside Les as he dialed the number. She could almost feel his heart beat wildly as he waited for Daphne to answer.

"Hello, Daphne, how are you today?" He asked trying to catch his breath.

"Well, Les Corbett, I am fine and how are you today?"

"Very well, thank you, I wondered if you would like to have…well go to …Uh…dinner tonight?"

"I suppose, well, yes I would what time?"

"I could pick you up about oh, well, about half past six?"

"That would be fine, at my shop?"

"Yes, at your shop, I will see you then." He said hanging up before she could hear his deep breathing.

"Well done, Les, you were awesome, now this is the best news I have had all year." She said resting the impulse to hug Les.

"I can't believe I just did that, I am stunned at what I just did."

"Now, you must remember to buy her some flowers."

"I will take lunch time to do that and what else?"

"Just relax, when you feel nervous just remember you are not alone, your best friend is with you." "You are going with us?"

"No, Les think about whom your best friend is…who does Richard talk about every Sunday?"

"Oh, Him. Of course, I will try to remember that, Hazel what would I have ever done without you…And Him?"

"We are all here to help each other, we are all brothers and sisters aren't we?"

"Yes I am beginning to believe that.'"

"Wear your navy jacket and gray slacks, you look good in them."

"I will and do you have any other advice your highness?"

"Be yourself, but not too much, you know, no rude songs or anything like that. Just remember you are a very intelligent and interesting person."

"Hazel, I owe you so much and before you go I have something for you to give to Richard." Les went to the back room and brought out the new three piece suit he had just finished for the vicar.

"Les, this is beautiful, Richard will be over the moon." She said.

"Let me know if he needs any alterations, I took very careful measurements and think it is going to fit well." He said smiling at the results.

"You can't imagine how much he needed a new suit."

"Oh yes I can I couldn't stand to see him in those old ones any longer and tell him I am going to make one more."

"How can we ever repay you? We just haven't had any extra money for suits."

"It makes me feel good for you to say that and to know I could repay you in such a small way for giving me back my life, actually saving my life."

"Take care Les and have a great night, we will keep you in our prayers." She smiled as she closed the door gently behind her.

CHAPTER TWENTY FIVE

Matt sorted through the newly purchased items from his last London trip to talk to Reggie Brooker.

He tried to cheer up and hope Anise would be giving her answer to his proposal soon.

He was certain she loved him but there was something holding her back from accepting the proposal.

He remembered the age routine he had heard all his childhood. She would continually call him Mattie and treat him like a toddler.

As he worked he tried to think of something to prove to her that she was not that much older than he was and her lingering answer had gone on long enough.

I will talk to Collin and see what we could come up with.

"Collin, are you busy tonight?"

"Well not really, Cinny has some meetings for the celebration and Lily and Reggie need her for something. What do you need?"

"Let's have dinner at the chip shop I need to talk to you, and need your help."

"I think I know what help you need and I don't know if I can but I will try. See you at seven there."

Matt phoned Reggie and asked if he would have lunch with him and try to get some insight from him before the talk with Collin that night.

"Reggie, will you have lunch with me?"

"Sure, I'll pick you up at one and I want you to take me to the commons to measure the moon and sea."

"Great, perfect timing, see you then."

The serene setting of the lush green area sat high on the white cliffs overlooking the village in one direction and the English Channel in the other was called the Commons. It was given to them by Captain Brooker in order for the community to have a recreational place for everyone to enjoy.

This was where the children and youth had their soccer field at one end and a football field on the other. In the center was where they would all come for picnics and parties. This was also where they would celebrate holidays such as' Guy Fawkes Night'. Every November fifth they would gather wood and make a cloth dummy in effigy of the man who failed in an attempt to assassinate King James I.

The old black sedan pulled up in front of the antique shop and Matt ran outside and slid in beside Reggie.

"Reggie, thank you for helping us out with our celebration and make it into a beautiful setting.

I hope you won't think I am strange but I have dreamed that one day I would make a paper moon and card board sea when I would dance with Anise and ask her to marry me.

The words from the lyrics of a song have stayed with me all through the war. When me and my squadron would fly at night and see the moon and the sea a song would play and replay in my thoughts.

Then when they talked about this party I knew this would be my chance to have everything come together. I knew I didn't have the talent to do it but then when we were in London I knew you could. Please don't share that with anyone, maybe Lily, but I don't want to become the town 'nutter'." He laughed.

"So you are going to ask Annie to marry you?"

"Actually, I already have but she is thinking about it."

"What is she thinking about? I can tell she likes you."

"I am three years younger than she is and I used to harass her on the playground when we were in school and she would call me Mattie and make me go away. Her friends would laugh and make fun of her with her little boy friend."

"I see, she is concerned about the age difference. I wouldn't have guessed you were younger if you hadn't told me."

"I know that is what I try to tell her and I promised I would take such good care of her that she would never age." He sighed.

"My boy be patient she will come around Lily and I will help, I think you two can be very happy."

"Thank you I need all the help I can get."

The two men walked to the area where the trees were where Matt thought the moon should hang from and place the cardboard underneath.

Reggie agreed it would be the perfect spot.

For the first time Matt could see everything come together in his life with his apprenticeship and Anise.

Collin waited for Matt to join him for dinner and went over to the juke box and put some coins in to play some of his favorite songs. One of them included 'Paper Moon'.

"What kept you? I was getting ready to call Cinny to have dinner with me."

"I had some ordering to do for the decorations and couldn't get through to the person I needed to talk to. Sorry. Have you ordered?" "Not yet. What did you need to talk about?"

"Well, Anise, have you heard anything from Cinny about what she has said about my proposal?"

"Not a word. Cinny promised anything Annie told her was in strict confidence."

"That is wonderful, well in a way; I don't know how I am going to get through this. I need to tell Antoine some general date when I will be there, but until Annie gives me her answer I can't go ahead with him finding a place for us to stay. I will have to make a deposit of some sort."

"Wish I had something to tell you but I don't, let's eat I am starved. I am almost through filling out all the papers for school. I will have to go to Oxford soon. Want to go with me?"

"Sure, let me know so I can get Josh to fill in for me and his friend."

"Have you and Cinny set a wedding date?"

"No, she wants to wait for Annie and see what she does about you.
Maybe we could have a double wedding?"

"Maybe, I only hope I will have a wedding."

"I think you will old boy, I have that gut feeling you will."

Collin laughed remembering how he and Matt would always talk about a gut feeling when something was good that they wanted to do.

CHAPTER TWENTY SIX

Nigel opened the storage door to get the boxes to stock shelves with Olive.

Suddenly he heard a noise.

"Who's there?"

"Nigel, it's me." Ron whispered.

"What are you doing here in the dark?"

"Shhh, Nigel, don't be so loud, just whisper. Is there a woman out there?"

"Yes, she is searching for bargains she said."

"Did she say how long she will be there?"

"No, why would she tell me how long she would be here?"

"Listen; please get rid of her for me. Is Olive out there?"

"Olive is out there making room for these boxes of canned goods I am supposed to bring to her. Why do I have to get rid of that woman?"

"Don't ask questions, just do it and I will tell you later. Please Nigel help me out."

"Oh, I see, you have been 'chatting' her up and she won't go away and Olive is there and…"

"Yes, you guessed it, I am in big trouble."

"You need to stop this you know, if you promise never to chat up another woman I will help you out this time but never again."

"Whatever you say Nigel, just get rid of her now."

"All right all right I'm going but this will be a bit 'dodgy'."

Nigel brought out the boxes from the store room as if nothing had happened and took them to Olive where she had made room for the contents.

"What took you so long?"

"I needed to get a drink of water, I was thirsty, sorry."

"That's O.K. Have you seen Ron?"

"No, I suppose he is making orders."

"I suppose so you may help the lady find her bargains."

"May I help you madam?"

"I am looking for your bargains, where is the gentleman that was here earlier?"

"He had to leave, won't be back for years."

"Where is he going?"

"He is ill and has to go to the hospital in London."

"That is awful, he looked healthy to me, but you never know about these things do you?"

"No, mam you never know about such things." He said escorting her to the door.

"She didn't find anything, Nigel?"

"No, she had to go she was late for something." He lied as he walked slowly to the store room again to let Ron know he could come out, that the woman had left.

Ron quietly slipped out of the storage room and out the back door to go to their house across the lawn from the shop.

He needed to get the order forms to fill out and make Nigel's lie into a truth.

Olive smiled as she reached for the phone in her living room with a new confidence of knowing her marriage was finally going in the right direction. That at last she was in control and would never have to experience that horrendous feeling her husband was unfaithful.

She had made up her mind she would never have to experience lack of confidence from feelings of rejection caused from watching Ron chat up every woman that would come into the store, when they were out to dinner, when they were with friends and even at church on Sundays.

This was going to be the beginning of the marriage she always wanted or she was going to leave him.

It brought such joy she could hardly contain herself and needed to talk to Anise and Cinny who had been the instigators of this plan to get her marriage on the right track or end it. "Annie, will you have lunch with me today?"

"Of course, do you have something to tell us?"

"Oh yes, it worked and have I got something funny to tell you about this morning. I will see you at noon."

As she sat gazing at the black phone she pictured her new look. She was going to do as the sisters advised. She would buy a new dress, get her hair cut and they were going to help her with makeup that they were wearing now every day.

All she could think about was how tired she was of her life. How tired she was of working morning until night six days a week, going to church on Sundays then home for the dinner she would always prepare to finish cooking on Sunday after church.

She was so depressed and tired of Ron that made her feel unworthy and ugly not allowing her to take her place as his wife and that he was still searching for someone to replace this woman so far beneath him and didn't fit what he needed in a wife.

The times she would shut herself in her bedroom after having to go through one of his flirtations and cried until she was exhausted and sick of her life. Tired of living a lowly life he had imposed upon her. She was so sick of his old routine she could hardly stand to look at him.

It had gotten so bad that she decided for self-defense she would have her own bedroom and he could do as he pleased, but not with her.

He had been shocked when she took him to the guest room one day several months before and opened the door then announced it was now her bedroom and he would have the one they had previously shared for the past ten years.

He had not acknowledged the separation; he had not said one word about it. It was as though he was in his own world and she was in hers. No communication, no conversations about anything personal between them or the demise of their relationship. Their conversations were only about the store, people in the village and some talk about their families and of course the ever present weather.

When they had gone together before they married they had a wonderful connection. They seemed to share the same opinions about life in general. He was complimentary to her and would tell her how pretty she was and how much he loved her and fortunate he was to have her in his life. He had made her feel wonderful and could hardly wait until they were married and start out their life together and have children.

When she could not conceive a child year after year it began to wear on them. The flirtations became more frequent and her self-esteem lower.

A few days earlier in the Brooker's Tea Shop she found it empty and Anise and Cinny sat with her and had tea and cakes and talked as she began to pour her heart out to them.

They came up with a plan to get back at Ron. At first Cinny wanted Olive to chat up the men around her as she saw her husband do with the ladies.

She couldn't picture herself doing that and rejected that idea.

Olive thought about her cousin Brenda who lived in Canterbury and he had never heard of nor met.

This was the woman Ron hid from when Nigel found him in the storage room earlier that day.

Olive observed her appearance in the bathroom mirror in her bedroom.

She had decided to have her hair cut that afternoon and had made the appointment the day before Brenda would start her part as the 'woman from hell' they laughed about it with Cinny and Anise.

The plan was for her to haunt him until he would be beaten down so much he would have to either tell her off or tell Olive what was going on.

The tea shop was busy as usual with the noon time customers and Olive and Cinny planned their lunch on the patio in the back for the lunch and be caught up with the latest part of their plan.

"Well, Olive tell us, what happened this morning?" Cinny asked.

Olive enjoyed telling her friends all the details of Ron and Nigel and how they tried to keep it from her.

"What is the next step?" Anise asked.

"Tonight the guys have the Home Guard meeting and Brenda will be waiting for him outside the door to surprise him.

"I can't wait to see what happens, I will call you and let you know. Brenda is going to get braver in her pursuit of him and even ask him to meet her later in the park. She is going to persist with different places to meet."

"How are you feeling about this Olive and what if he takes her up on these meetings?" Cinny wanted to know.

"I am tired of the life I am living and this will give me the conclusion or a new start in my marriage. I can't handle it any longer. I have been so tired and lonely it would better if I were actually single and not have to worry about what he was doing and who he was doing it with. It has to end one way of the other."

"I am so sorry you have to go through this. We are here if you need us at any time of the day or night. Phone or come over if you ever need us." Anise said softly.

"Yes, Olive and don't worry we will not and have not told anyone about this plan."

"Thank you both, now I must be off, I have an appointment to get my hair cut. Tonight we are going to work with the make up?"

"Yes, come when you can we will get everything ready."

"Thank you again for everything what would I have done without you both?"

"No bother, we know you would help us if we needed help. Let's enjoy it and see what happens. I know the outcome will be the right one which ever one it is."

Olive walked swiftly from the patio down the street to 'Marva's Beauty Shop' not wanting anyone to see her. This was the first time she had ever been inside one let along actually getting her hair done professionally.
With a fresh new outlook on her life Olive opened the door to the salon hopefully to the life with Ron she had hoped for so many years ago.

CHAPTER TWENTY SEVEN

The men in the Home Guard squadron gathered in the town hall on the Thursday night at seven o'clock.

Tully called them to order and they all stood in a long row as usual as he called them to attention.

His usual inspection of their guns and at intervals would have one of them take their weapon apart to see if it was clean and in proper working order.

He could sense the finality of their need to protect the village and the beach front.

The lingering feeling of self-preservation from the enemy was finally diminishing and he could also tell the men were coming to the same conclusion.

This was early June and they were finally able to feel their fears moving into acceptance that the war was truly over.

Their only concern was that Japan still had not given up their warfare in the Pacific and until then there was the need to stay watchful and on guard.

"I have the new schedules for the next month and if any of you have any reason you are not able to fulfill your part please let me know as soon as you can. No later than tomorrow so that I may be able to re organize everyone.

I am sure you all are having the same thoughts I am that soon we will not have to do this but for now until we see what happens with Japan we need to continue with our routines and not take a chance of being caught off guard."

"Tully, I have to take a trip to France for a few days so please fill my spot until I return." Matt said.

"Thank you for letting me know so soon, I will and let me know when you do come back and I will fit you in another part of the schedule, anyone else can let me know tonight?"

The men stood quietly shaking their heads no and that they were able to complete their schedule.

The guards disassembled to the long table to talk about their schedule and share their plans for the future and things happening in their lives at the moment.

"Ron, there is someone waiting for you at the front door." Collin whispered into his ear.

"What?"

Collin told him again quietly there was a woman waiting for him at the front door so the other men could not hear what he said.

"I have to leave." Ron said getting up and ran out the back door.

"What was that all about?" Matt asked.

"I don't know. Guess he had something to do." Collin said not wanting to draw attention to the woman waiting outside the front door for their friend.

Ron ran as fast as he could until he got home and hurriedly opened the door and ran upstairs to his room.

Olive sat in the living room by the fireplace as the fire dwindled down to bright orange coals.

She had been completely immersed in the new novel she recently bought on her book club list.

Hardly able to restrain her laughter she walked up the stairs and tapped on his door to ask him if he was all right.

Knowing what had happened she gained her composure and asked "Ron are you all right?"

"Yes, come in."

"The way you ran up the stairs I was afraid there was someone after you. Are you sure you are O.K.?"

"I'm fine, just tired, I need to get up early in the morning to rearrange the store room. We need more space. Did you do something with your hair?"

"My hair?"

"Yes, you look different, did you cut it?"

"Oh, that, yes, I went to the salon. I was tired of long hair; it takes too long to dry. I will let you get some sleep now you look tired, see you tomorrow." She said softly closing the door before he could say anything else.

Ron lay in his empty bed feeling uneasy about the last two days of the woman that was pursuing him. He had never had that happen before. The women he would flirt with never took him serious until now. It frightened him to think this woman could mean trouble for him and give everyone especially Olive the wrong impression.

He knew he was losing Olive and he didn't know what he could do to get her back.

There were the feelings she wasn't in love with him anymore. The question was what he could do to make their marriage the way it had been when they were first married.

He had to talk to someone; he supposed it would have to be the vicar, he would phone him tomorrow.

Not able to sleep Ron got up at five o'clock and went to the shop and began moving the new shipment that came the day before to the newly built shelves in the back room located on the wall across from the storage room.

Each order became easier to obtain and didn't have to wait as long as just a few months ago.

He had decided to expand as much as he could with the amount of space he had and utilizing wall space as much as possible building shelves to hold all the shipments he planned to have.

New products he wanted to try, as well as more variety in normal orders such as produce and canned goods that was beginning to be more available.

All of a sudden there was a tap on the window and he could barely see the shadow of a woman…the woman he had been running from.

He slid down on the floor behind the door that was partly opened which separated the front of the shop and crawled through to the storage area and small office in the back.

He held his breath listening to her tap on the window again.

Before he knew what happened Olive came through the back door and found him on his knees hiding from the woman that his wife knew nothing about.

"Ron, what are you doing on your knees?"

"Shhhh, be quiet."

"Why, what's wrong?"

"Nothing, there is a woman wanting to come in and I just wanted to get some work done and didn't want to open now." He said proud of himself coming up with the excuse why he was acting so strange.

"I'll wait on her; we need all the business we can get." She said going to the front door and opening it.

"Hello, may I help you?" Olive asked Brenda winking without Ron seeing her.

"Yes, I needed some bread." She said smiling and looking around to see where Ron might be.

"Ron, could you bring some bread up to the front?"

There was no answer and she went to the back and to her amazement he had fled.

"He's gone, I have never seen him move so quickly before, and this is a new Ron." Olive laughed quietly just in case he might be close.

Brenda bought the bread and left going on with the plan they had contrived.

Finally reaching the church door he whipped open the door to the office.

"Vicar, I need to talk to you, do you have some time today, this morning by any chance?" Ron asked out of breath.

"Yes, I do, are you all right Ron?"

"I am fine I only need to talk to you see you at ten."

"Well, sure, see you at ten."

Ron with slouched shoulders walked slowly back up the hill to his waiting wife.

Olive watched her nervous husband unpack the boxes and carefully move everything to their proper place. A few minutes to ten he told her he had another delivery to make to the vicar and would be back shortly.

He walked swiftly down the hill once more to the vicarage with an eerie feeling someone was following him.

Thinking it was the woman he started to run as fast as he could for cover.

He felt like a deer being stalked during hunting season.

"Ron, are you hiding from someone? What's going on?"

"I don't know but I think someone is following me. Can we go into your office and lock the door?"

"Sure, but I don't think locking the door is necessary, suit yourself." Richard said sitting behind his large mahogany desk with the green library lamp.

The smell of polished wood lingered through the book filled room.

Ron had not noticed until now the sea of books the vicar had pertaining to the bible written by authors both old and new with several versions and accounts of ancient prophets.

"Now, Ron tell me what's going on. You are acting strange."

Ron made an in-depth account of the last few days with the woman that was stalking him and ending with a plea for help out of the situation.

"Ron, you know you have this coming to you. I have seen you 'chat' women up and wondered when Olive would get enough of it and leave you. I can't believe you are so hard hearted to do this to her. You do realize how much it hurts her?"

"No, I never thought about that, it was just a game I liked to play when I was bored, that's all."

"That is the worst excuse I have ever heard, bored? Just because you had nothing better to do you flirted with women and made your wife feel less of a person, but because you were bored?"

"Hold on, you don't have to get so angry."

"Angry…how dare you even attempt to excuse yourself. You are despicable I have wanted to talk to you for years but felt it wasn't my business. Now I see there was no need the good Lord saw to it you fell into the pit you dug yourself and now you need my help getting out."

"Enough of the guilt you may give me a sermon later right now there is a woman lurking in the bushes and the shop waiting for me."

"Serves you right, what can I do about her?"

"Tell her to leave me alone, not to bother me again."

"You sound like a frightened little boy Ron. Grow up and face this like a man. You brought this on now you fix it. Running away from her won't solve the problem. Talk to her and tell her you are a married man and she needs to stop following you. She will, I am sure you don't have the magnetism that drives women wild." He said chuckling at the pale faced parishioner.

"You mean all I have to do is tell her to go away and leave me alone and she will?"

"Yes, I am telling you that is all you have to do, it is a very simple way to face your problem."

"What if she won't?"

"Then you come back to me and I will help you convince her."

"All right but I wish you would stay with me and help me when I see her again so I can hurry and get this over with."

"Only if she won't listen to you the first time, by the way are you coming to Sunday service?"

"Yes, of course I am always there you see me don't you?"

"I do, but evidently nothing I have ever said did you any good. It looks like either my sermons were not affective or you slept through them."

"I guess I didn't apply them to me, but from now on I am going to listen."

"Good, open your ears and it will amaze you what you actually hear." Richard laughed.

"I will let you know what happens hopefully I will be through this by tomorrow, hopefully tonight."

"I will wait for you to call if you need my help."

Ron walked slowly up the hill to his grocery shop passing all the familiar stores on his way noticing how everyone was busy cleaning the sidewalks and washing windows.

"Ron, where have you been?"

"Oh, just had an order to deliver to Mrs. Wilson. What do you need?"

"Oh, nothing, just wondered why you slipped away."

"I didn't slip away; I told you I had a delivery."

"You sure disappeared quickly. Are you sure you are all right?"

"I am fine, just want to speed up all the orders I can, now that the war is over we will be able to make some money and maybe take a trip...you have always wanted to go to Paris, what do you think about that?"

"Ron, that would be wonderful, whatever made you think of a trip?"

"Oh, I don't know, maybe it was your new hairdo." He sighed hoping she would accept his plan for a trip and forget about his odd behavior.

Brenda waited outside the grocery shop for Ron to come out and sweep the sidewalk at this time of day.

Ron grabbed the broom and started to sweep and suddenly saw the woman who had been chasing him.

"What do you want young lady?"

Ron said trying to remain calm.

"I wanted to talk to you about maybe, well…maybe dinner at my place?"

"I am a married man and I love my wife, you have to stop following me, now go away and don't come back." He said quietly not wanting to bring attention to his malady.

"I thought you were interested in me the way you chatted

me up." Brenda tried to control herself and not laugh.

"You thought wrong, now go away now and never come back." He whispered coming closer to her.

"I suppose, but I think you are a very handsome man and thought we could have dinner and get more acquainted." She continued.

"I said go, now, I don't want you around here anymore, go before I call the police." He said as quietly as he could. His heart pounded so loud he could hardly hear her.

"Oh, all right, but you'll be sorry when I am gone, we could have had a wonderful time together." She said leaving Ron to sweep the sidewalk and to go home after her job well done.

CHAPTER TWENTY EIGHT

Matt and Collin walked along the beach as the sunset washed its last glow over the water giving the area and them the feeling they were in golden globe. "Have you heard from Anise?"

Collin asked.

"Not a word, Cinny won't talk to me about what her answer might be. I'm not sure what to do. It can't be that hard to talk to me and let me know what she is feeling at least so we could talk about it. If I don't hear from her tonight I am going to the shop tomorrow and if I have to throw her over my shoulder to talk to her one way or the other."

"I don't know what else you can do, so may I watch?" Collin laughed.

"Sure, I can use all the support I can get even if it is a good laugh."

"Let's go to the tea shop and see if they are still open. Sometimes they stay later in the summer."

"Good ideal"

The two friends climbed the sandy hill back up to the village.

"They are there, wonderful luck." Matt said.

Anise and Cinny brought out the last order of the day to the waiting customers not aware Matt and Collin slip in the side door and sat down by the window overlooking the Channel.

"Where did you come from?" Anise asked.

"Let me see, I came from Brooker's Village-On-Sea, on the southern shore of England. How about you Collin?"

"I was born in a cabbage patch if you must know." He laughed nervously.

"We are busy but did you need something?"

"Yes, I need you." Matt smiled.

"Please, there are people around, be quiet. We will be with you shortly. Help yourself to some tea and whatever else you want." She said leaving quickly before Matt made any other smart comment. "Well, at least I will get an answer tonight one way or the other."

"I wouldn't rush anything, let her take her time. If you push her she will shut you out of her life. Allow her room to feel comfortable about a decision."

"I know, you are right I am just trying to get things organized to leave for France after the celebration."

"I understand, even knowing Cinny will marry me I am having trouble getting things in place. Remember to talk softly to her and not get upset and show anger or you will push her away."

"I will, thank you for your help, I'll miss you. Maybe someday you will be able to set up your practice here in the village. Have you thought that far in advance?"

"As a matter of fact, George asked me if I would like to join him in his practice when I am ready. I told him yes."

"That is good news, you will have your practice and I will have my boat business."

Anise and Cinny cleaned off the last table and set the rest of the dishes in the kitchen for Polly and the others to finish the cleanup.

Untying her apron Anise sat down across from Matt and Collin and then Cinny joined them.

"You look like you are up to something." Anise said.

"That is a laugh, what could I be up to?" Matt chuckled.

"How should I know, you look guilty, tell me what you are planning?"

"I don't know about Collin, but I can't make any plans until you give me the answer to my question."

"Let's talk about that privately, will you wait for me and then we will talk."

"Collin, why don't you and Matt come home with me and wait for us there?"

Collin took Cinny by the arm and walked slowly to the cottage while Matt walked ahead of them hurrying to hopefully find out as soon as he could the answer he was in hopes of hearing.

Matt walked around the cottage trying to keep his energy level up and be as alert as he could manage.

The cushiony dark sky was pinned with sparkling stars that brought out the splendor of the endless universe.

Matt began to relax and was beginning to feel at ease in spite of the pending answer he had waited so long to hear.

The stone walk around Anise's home was well worn and perfectly trimmed. The bright thick lawn was immaculately mowed up to the winding flowering boarders that touched and followed the towering dark green hedges which made a natural fence that enhanced the lovely white cottage.

He hadn't realized what a beautiful setting it was with the Brooker's home overlooking the Channel which added to the beautiful painting worthy of any gifted artist.

"Matt, there you are, I have been looking for you. Sorry I kept you waiting." Anise said out of breath.

"I was just enjoying your lawn and gardens and your view is spectacular. Almost as beautiful as you are." He smiled taking her hand.

"Matt, I'm sorry I have been ignoring you this past week but I was completely caught off guard when you proposed.

I wasn't surprised when Collin asked Cinny to marry him but you... well I was..."

"That is all right, I hadn't planned to ask you that night, it just came out. I have loved you for so many years I couldn't wait another minuet to let you know how serious I feel about you."

"Let's walk down to the beach so we can have some privacy, I don't want anyone to interrupt us. We need to get things settled once and for all."

"That doesn't sound very romantic; you sound like a school teacher.
I guess I don't have a choice so I am in your hands so be gentle."

"I didn't realize how dramatic you are little Mat... oops."

Matt grabbed her and kissed her keeping his promise that each time she called him Mattie he would kiss her.

"All right, all right, sorry." She said trying to breathe.

Continuing her intended conversation she said." Matt, I don't know what to say to your proposal. For now at least I cannot say yes. All I can tell you is that maybe someday... but don't count on it. I can't see myself married to anyone and especially to someone younger than I am. I don't want to end up becoming your old hag. I'm sorry, I can't marry you."

Matt's jaw was clenched as well as his fists wanting something to hit but nothing around at the moment so the next option was to remain quiet.

The silence was overwhelming as Anise waited for a response but instead he led her back to the cottage and opened the door let her go inside then he left without saying a word.

He drove back to his house around the corner from the antiques shop he had worked in all his life.

In a trance Matt would not allow himself feel the cutting words he had heard from the love of his life.

The pain he was trying to ignore began to seep deeper into his heart and he went down stairs into the basement where the little 'make shift' gym where the punching bag was hanging.

He started to punch it and then again and again until he was wet from sweat and exhausted.

He took a long hot shower wanting to relax so he would be able to sleep off the painful ordeal he had just experienced.

In all the time he was in active duty in France he had never been through anything as excruciating as the finality that there would be no wedding.

Instead the experience was as if someone ripped his heart from his chest and threw it out in the waves as they washed upon the sand.

He crawled into the oversized feather bed he had slept in ever since he could remember.

Instead of sleep only echoes of painful words bounced around the walls of the wood paneled bedroom. Tossing and turning, he finally got up and went down stairs to get a glass of milk to help him sleep.

Pacing on the well-worn paisley wool rug he knew he could not sleep so he put on his clothes and went for a walk.

He made up his mind he would go to Collin's and see if he had anything to help him sleep.

He knocked on the door and finally it opened and saw his friend yawning and stretching envious of his ability to sleep.

"Hi, sorry to bother you, do you have anything to help me get some sleep?"

"Sure, come in, why did you leave us so suddenly? Did Anise say no?"

"Yes, she said no. I never want to hear her name again. I am leaving for France tomorrow. Uncle Reggie and Aunt Lily can finish the decorations we are almost ready for the party. They don't need me now. I just want to get a good night's sleep and leave as soon as I can."

"I'm sorry it turned out this way, but happy you have something to go to and put your heart and soul into."

"Yeah, well, I have something to put my energy into making boats and that is good enough for me. I am grateful I don't have to stay here and any longer. I want to get on with my life."

"Here are some tablets they will help you. They don't need a prescription, I only keep over the counter medications so don't worry, and they are safe.

I have your address so I will keep in touch with you; please let me know how you are doing and when you will be back. Sorry you won't be here for the big celebration, I was looking forward to watching you dance with Anise under the paper moon you and Reggie made."

"I don't ever want to hear those words again and I am not joking about it, don't ever say those words again." He winced.

"She must have cut you deeply. Your wounds are showing, sorry old man. I can't tell you how awful I feel about this. I will miss you and please write, promise?"

"I will write and thanks for the tablets see you in a year."

Matt walked with slumped shoulders and hands shoved in his pockets walked down the dimly lit sidewalk to his house to try once again to get some sleep after he packed and got ready to leave as soon as he could on the ferry to France.

The next morning found the sun hidden in gray clouds that held it hostage

The colorless sky matched Anise's mood as she tried to shake off the dark feelings from the conversation and swift departure of Matt the night before.

She was stunned from his lack of response and his sudden departure before saying one word after she had refused his proposal.

She went through the motions of getting ready to go to work.

Cinny was humming as she put a pan of buns in the oven. She and Collin had made more plans the night before for their move to Oxford. She was going to take classes while he was going to medical school. She wanted to become a teacher. At least take classes to keep her busy."

"You sound cheerful this dreary morning."

"I am, how did last night go with Matt?"

"I have no idea." She said looking down into the sink piled with dirty pans.

"Are you all right Annie?"

"I don't know. I told Matt last night I couldn't marry him. When I finished telling him how I felt he brought me home and without saying one word left and went home.

"Oh, Annie, you hurt him deeply. You need to talk to him and see how he is doing today. That is not like him at all."

Walking as fast as she could down the long hill to the side by side shops Annie was out of breath when she reached the Rutledge shop.

She opened the front door as the bell tinkled its usual sound and looked around for Matt. Josh came to the front.

"Hi Josh, is Matt here?"

"Oh, no, he left for France early this morning, didn't you know?"

"No he didn't tell me."

"Did he tell you about his apprenticeship with the Frenchman learning how to make boats?"

"No, that is a total surprise, when did that happen?"

"He has planned this since he came home. He was going to tell you all about it."

"I have to go Josh, but will you give me his address where he will be staying please?"

"Sure, let me get some paper." He said scribbling down the information.

Anise ran back up the hill to the shops where Cinny was looking for her.

"Annie I didn't know you left and I have been looking all over for you."

"Cinny, Matt left for France. He is going to live there and be an apprentice to a boat maker, can you believe that?"

"That is some news and did you know he was going to do that?"

"No, maybe he was going to tell me last night when I said no to his proposal. I feel awful.

I really hurt him Cinny."

"You can go see him but let him get settled and then go find him after the celebration."

"I will, I have so much to do for the celebration and our food order and then make a reservation for where ever it is he is living." Annie sighed then the tears came not able to hold them back.

Cinny put her arms around her sobbing sister leading her to the kitchen.

"Annie, you can't just leave now, calm down and pull yourself together. We will find a way to get in touch with him without you going over there now; we have too many obligations at this time. This doesn't sound like you, let's sit down and have some tea and sort this all out. This isn't like you at all, listen to yourself…you love him don't you?"

"No…oh, I don't know, I didn't…well I had no idea until I found out he left for France and had all these plans and didn't have any idea he was going to live there and be in an apprenticeship with of all things making boats. He always loved airplanes now this sudden change. I feel so lost."

"Let's talk about this and I am going to call Hazel, do you mind?"

"I don't mind, she might have some good advice. I'll make breakfast while you talk to her and ask Polly if she will take over and prepare for lunch customers."

"I will, be back shortly."

Annie started to make breakfast for them and turned the radio on when she heard the tune that penetrated her heart as she listened to "Paper Moon".

She tried to avoid the deep emotion the song brought to her heart as she turned the radio off.

Her mood darkening the tears returned as she finished the meal she set on the table and slumped down in the chair beside the window overlooking the Channel water Matt had recently traveled to start his new life.

The gray sky infused the water with its dull hue which blended with her mood that minute by minute was becoming darker.

"I am glad you are back, what took you so long?"

"Hazel had to phone me back because the vicar had to use it, so I had to wait for her to call back. Are you all right?"

"No, I am not, this darkness is worsening. I have never felt like this before. Even when mum and dad died something told me everything was all right and they were in a good place and we would never have to worry about them again. This is new for me; I can't make it go away. Nothing is helping. What did Hazel say is she coming over?"

"She is coming and should be here by now. Look, the sun is peeking through the clouds."

The sisters sat across the table from each other staring out the window waiting to discuss the persisting dark mood with their surrogate mother, Hazel Grovenor.

The sound of the door knocker let them know their visitor had arrived.

"Hazel, thank you so much for being so prompt, are you ready for breakfast?"

"Yes, thank you I am hungry after the walk up the hill faster than my normal pace." She said taking off her blue felt hat that was the only one she owned.

"Sit down Hazel, let me take your hat and set it up for you on the shelf."

The three women sat and talked and ate as the sun began to shine through the kitchen window filling them and the room with warmth and hope for Annie's future.

CHAPTER TWENTY NINE

The chatter in the town hall grew louder as the Ladies Auxiliary celebration committee's chairmen and their assistants started to resolve the issues that had transpired through the week since their last meeting.

Lucy Burkhart and Missy Odette's committee discussed the talent show and who would be participating and what they would be doing. Their largest problem was to find professional groups or individuals they could afford that would fit in within a family setting filling out the evening's entertainment.

"I did find a magician we would be able to afford and he lives in Woldford. What do you think?"

"I think that is a wonderful idea. Have you talked to him?"

"No, not yet I wanted to talk to Hazel first and the rest of the committee."

"Is this what he does for a living or just a hobby?"

"Oh, it is his occupation. He is wonderful I have seen him make things disappear."

"I think that would be horrible to say your husband is a magician and makes things disappear. Mind you, my husband makes things disappear, 'Yorkshire Pudding', 'Shepard's Pie', Apple Tarts with Custard." Lucy chuckled.

They all laughed he would be a good talent but not their idea of a proper occupation for their husbands.

Ron and Phil's committee that was in charge of the carpenters, electricians, and other skilled crews shared their similar problems that no one seemed to be in charge and they were not organized and weren't sure what they were supposed to be doing. The two men had to organize the men and skills so they could set the ground work that would allow the decoration committee uses the builders and electricians to erect their projects.

"Please everyone, quiet, we have lots of work to do. I will ask each chairman to stand and give a report, and problems we need to resolve. We will start with Missy and go around the table, I will take notes so speak clearly and let me have time to have so I can have a clear understanding of what you need help with. We would like to start with Ron and Phil to give their report as they found they will be the foundation of all the committees. If any of you have questions for them wait until the end of all the reports and then ask in individual groups so we may get an idea of how far we have come and be able to calendar the date of the celebration, time is running out, we don't want to wait until fall because of weather. So Ron and Phil please stand and give your report."

The committees gave an account of what had been done so far, their needs and when they felt they would finish.

Annie and Cinny sat next to their Uncle Reggie and Aunt Lily to ask them questions about Matt's sudden disappearance.

"Uncle Reggie, how are you doing with the art work and how has it been since Matt left?"

"We are doing fine, Lily and I are getting help from the youth and everything is on target. We want to finish our work so we can move from London to your small cottage. Did Matt talk to you about that?"

"You and Aunt Lily are moving here?"

"Yes, I thought you knew, didn't Matt tell you our plan while his is going through his apprenticeship in France?"

"No, he didn't he had all this planned without our knowledge?"

"You don't like us moving here?"

"Oh, I think that is wonderful, Dad would be very happy you would live here. It is just such a surprise."

"Didn't you talk to him before he left?"

"No, he left suddenly …"

"She turned down his proposal Uncle Reggie." Cinny said.

"Oh, that says it all. Sorry, guess we won't have to move after all."

"I don't know what your plans were with him, but we would love to have you live here with us, the cottage would be perfect for your studio, but please we have plenty of room in our cottage for you to live, how does that sound?"

"Well, Lily, what do you think?"

The small woman with large eyeglasses that continually rested on her small nose looked up and joined the conversation from her reserved by stander position said "I think that would be very nice. Are you sure we wouldn't be in your way actually living in the same cottage with you?"

"We have plenty of room and we would love your company, it has been so empty since mum and dad passed away."

"Thank you, Reggie, I think it would be nice to live with them, I love the view of the Channel and want to paint it someday."

"The small cottage would make a great studio, and it has a good view as well. We can leave our address and phone number for our London customers. We will also leave that information with our friends there as well at the shops so we won't lose business."

"Everyone, we will close the meeting and there are refreshments tonight from Ron and Olive Simon. Thank you both for the wonderful table you set up for us. Remember if you have questions please use this time to go to the chairman and ask whatever you need from them. Les, will you ask the blessing on the food?"

The food was blest from the repentant Les Corbett and the hall spread out with groups of coordinating each other with questions and resolves.

The village was becoming more relaxed and letting go of their protective vigil of war time and starting to enjoy their new peacetime life.

CHAPTER THIRTY

Tully drove under the 'Applegates Farm 'sign that swung from the high white washed posts that stood over the road leading the two miles up to the Gates' farm house.

He rounded the curve to the house watching Marilee and Wesley running from the shed that was billowing with thick smoke from the windows and door that clouded Rob, Ry and Homer's run for fresh air to breathe after the miss fire of their homemade fireworks they were working on for the celebration.

Watching the animals run as far away as they could for protection the whole farm was in a loud commotion.

Tully knocked on the back door and Phil swung it open trying to reach the fracas as soon as possible.

"Hi Tully come with me we have some animals taking off from the blast from the boys shed." He laughed used to this kind of emergency.

"Are they all right?"

"You mean the boys?"

"Yes."

"They are fine, I just need to keep the animals from escaping, help me?"

"Sure, does this happen often?"

"Oh, every once in a while, more now they are trying to get ready for the celebration. I told them we should just buy them but they want to contribute their inventions."

Phil and Tully ran around the farm ushering animals back to their pens.

"Thank you Tully for the help stay for supper?"

"Thank you I will, I worked up quite an appetite."

The two men slowly walked back to the house enjoying the more relaxed atmosphere.

"Irene, I invited Tully for dinner, set an extra plate."

"Hello, Tully, of course, Marilee please get him a plate. You two can wash up, you both look hot and sweaty." She smiled and winked at her husband.

The long dining room table was covered with the old lace cloth saved for company and the best china was brought out as Marilee and Wesley set the table for everyone including Rob, Ryan and Homer.

"Everyone come and eat, dinner is ready." Irene called.

After the blessing on the food they started passing their plates for Phil to start filling them with the tender pot roast.

"This is perfect timing, I love your Yorkshire Pudding Irene. Thank you for allowing me to join you tonight." Tully said.

"You are so welcome, you must be tired from gathering the animals, I saw you and Phil running all over the farm did you get them all sorted out and back in their right places?" She chuckled.

"We did my love, thanks to Tully. The boys helped as well."

"Don't forget Wesley and I did too, after those…oh…pass the green beans." Marilee coughed.

"Yes, Marilee, you need to put your hand over your mouth when you cough, remember that."

Irene shot the well knowing look to her sarcastic daughter.

"I will mummy, I forgot."

"Don't forget again."

"Tully, how is Ivy doing? Will she sing in the talent show?"

"I don't know, I am trying to convince her to say yes."

"Maybe you could get Les Corbett and Nigel to help. They are in charge of the music and could maybe work with her and let her practice on the stand."

"That is a great idea, Irene, I will suggest that to her."

"I didn't know she could sing." Marilee said.

"She has a beautiful voice; we all have been surprised with her gift."

"Are you going to get married?" Marilee asked Tully.

"What?"

"Are you going to marry Ivy?"

"I don't know, why?"

"M…." She coughed slapping her hand over her mouth.

"Marilee, please go upstairs and clear your throat."

Marilee ran upstairs to get herself under control before she would be in trouble.

"That was awkward." Wesley said.

"Marilee has recently been having trouble with allergies. All of a sudden she just started to have them.

"Yeah, she…" Wesley stopped after he felt a kick from his mother under the table.

"Tully, is everything going all right with your committee?"

Irene asked trying to take the focus off Marilee.

"We are doing well now that Phil and I are organizing the ground crew."

The evening meal went smoothly and the conversation stayed on the celebration and centered on help from Robert, Ryan and Homer for the next few days.

Tully drove home slowly with thoughts of Ivy and the out of the blue question about his relationship with her.

This was the first inclination he had that the village was talking about their dates and if there were a permanent relationship in the future.

Driving by the chemist shop Ivy would probably have left he wondered if she was in storage room playing and singing.

He parked the old brown truck covered with dirt from the trip to the Gates farm.

He knocked on the door loudly but not wanting to draw attention.

The door opened and Ivy welcomed him inside and closed the door quickly.

"What are you doing here?"

"I am checking to see if you are practicing your music you will be singing at the celebration." He smiled down at her flushed face.

"Well, I was singing but not to perform at the talent show." She said looking up at him trying not to lose her composure.

"I have an idea, come let's go to the storage room" He said leading her by the hand. "What idea?"

"Well, why don't we ask Les and Nigel to help you overcome your stage fright?"

"Les and Nigel?"

"Yes, I am sure if we ask them they will be able to help and give you some ideas to do to overcome this. They are both very accomplished musicians."

"Let me think about it, I can't imagine what they could do to help. I'll think about it though. What are you doing out this late at night?"

"I had dinner with Phil and Irene and their family. It was very interesting conversation, you should have been there."

"What was so interesting?"

"They wanted to know about our relationship and if I was going to marry you?"

"Marry me?"

"Yes, how about it?"

"What are you talking about, marrying me?"

"Well after I left their house I thought that was a good idea."

"What was a good idea?"

She asked frowning and totally confused.

"Getting married, how about it?"

"How about it?"

"Ivy, stop repeating what I am saying, will you marry me?"

"How did we go from me overcoming my stage fright to getting married?"

"I don't know it just happened."

"Stop dodging the question, will you marry me?"

"I don't know, do I have to tell you this minute?"

"Tomorrow, tell me tomorrow. That will be soon enough, I have to know tomorrow, will that be all right?"

"I suppose, I will try and give you an answer tomorrow. I don't know why it can't wait for a while and let me take some time. This is sudden."

"I know, sorry, it just happened so fast with the question at the Gates' dinner table."

"I will promise to give you an answer tomorrow, how about dinner tomorrow night?"

"I will pick you up here at six when you close for dinner?"

"No, pick me up at seven at home so I can freshen up."

"Wonderful, I will see you then, at seven…"

He chuckled as he left her in the storage room and let himself out side where the dark blue sky gave the stars a velvet background.

CHAPTER THIRTY ONE

Annie and Cinny hurried to the teashop that bright morning after sleeping in to their dismay.

"I can't believe we slept in, hope Polly and Audrey are there and have everything under control.

Jerking the back door open to the kitchen they were relieved to see everyone rushing around preparing breakfast for the waiting customers.

"Thank you everyone, you are wonderful. We will reward you for this. We can't thank you enough."

Annie and Cinny said hugging them for saving the early meal for the truant owners.

When the kitchen was clean after the morning customers Annie and Cinny sat at the small table fitted by the window that gave them their favorite view.

"I don't know why I am so tired, Cinny. I can't get enough sleep lately. I used to fall asleep as soon my head hit the pillow now I toss and turn and maybe after two I can sleep but get up exhausted."

"I think until you talk to Matt you will not be able to relax. Don't you agree?"

"Well, maybe, I don't know what else is causing it."

"Talk to Hazel and find out if everything is on track with the food so you can take a quick trip to France and straighten everything out with Matt."

"I will let's take a bike ride down to the vicarage. Let's get Polly to come in while we are gone."

The sisters rode slowly and carefully down the hill on their old worn bicycles.

"What are you going to say when you see Matt?"

"I don't know, probably cry."

"Do you think you will be able to find him?"

"I am worried, will you go with me?"

"Should we both be gone at the same time?"

"We could ask Uncle Reggie and Aunt Lily to oversee Polly and the rest if they need any help.

"I think that would work."

"Hope Hazel is home I hate to think we have to walk the bikes back up the hill for nothing."

They parked the rusty bikes and walked to the door."

"Hello girls, what are you doing here?"

"We needed to talk to you about the celebration. Do you have a few minutes?"

"Yes, of course come in. I'll ask Bea to bring us tea."

"We needed to know if the food is under control and everything listed we want to do for the night. We want to take a quick trip to France before that night but didn't want to leave if you needed us for anything?"

"I think you and I and the rest of the food committee have it taken care of and have thought it through what will be wanted and needed. Why are you going to France?"

"Well, we haven't been sleeping very well lately and thought a nice little trip to France might help us relax." Cinny smiled at her surprised sister at her quick wit and not quite telling a lie.

"How long will you be gone?"

"Not more than a few days, not even a week." Annie added.

"We need to be going and thank you for all you do for us Hazel. Our village has so much to thank you for now only the celebration organization but the individual help you give us all."

"You are welcome, but I need no thanks, I love this village and all who reside here. I hope you have a nice trip and get some rest and come back rested. By the way tell Matt hello for me."

She said smiling at their surprised faces.

The sisters walked to their bikes and pedaled carefully wanting to leave the church yard as soon as possible to talk about their sudden realization Hazel knew full well why they wanted to go for a quick trip to France.

"Cinny, I don't know, I don't feel good about taking the trip, I am going to see what happens, maybe he will come back for the celebration, I am not going, and I am going to work as hard as I can and drink warm milk before bedtime and try to get some sleep."

"It is up to you 'sissy'. I will do what you want to do and what you feel is the best to handle this, it is your life, I have mine sorted out so I am here for you if you need me."

"Thank you and that is the first time you've called me that in years."

"I know, I am really feeling a change coming in our lives. Uncle Reggie and Aunt Lily coming to live here, me move in a few weeks to Oxford and you...well..."

"Left alone...is that what you are trying to say?"

"Well, yes, but not alone exactly...only without...Matt."

"I suppose time will heal all wounds and mine will heal one way or the other. I also know my life will work out the way it should."

"Let's go home take a hot bath do our hair, and go out to dinner at the Beach Front and then go to the movies. I want to see the new one with Vivian Leigh."

"I will check with Collin first and see what he is doing, all right?"

"Of course, we can go by the shop on our way home."

The girls took their bicycles to the back of the Jarvis Chemist Shop and knocked on the back door.

"What are you two doing knocking on the back door?"

"We wanted to put our bicycles here out of the way we are tired of pushing them up the hill can we leave them here for now?" Cinny asked Collin.

"Yes, certainly I'll lock them up in the shed before I go home. What are you doing here?"

"I was wondering what you, or rather we were doing tonight, if anything?"

"I hadn't gotten that far, we have had a very busy day with new inventory and salesmen and customers, why?"

"Annie wanted to go to the movies and I wanted to go with her. Just wanted to let you know what we were doing." Cinny smiled.

"Sure, I could use some quiet time. Did you know Matt is coming home tomorrow?"

"Really, did he say why?"

"No, just that he had some business to take care of." Collin winked.

"We will be going so will see you tomorrow." Cinny said kissing Collin on the cheek.

"That was remarkable, what timing, I knew we shouldn't plan on the trip to France. Wonder how long he will be here?" Annie asked.

"I have no idea and that was very interesting. I can't wait to see what he is going to do and how long he will be here."

The sisters walked up the long hill to the Brooker's Tea Shop chatting and laughing forgetting how tired they had been before they stopped at the chemist shop.

Matt quickly boarded the ferry that would take him home. He had decided after talking it over with the old Frenchman he should go home and mend his broken heart by talking things over with Annie. This time he would use more patience and wisdom than he had shown when he abruptly left for his new life.

Traveling from the south up to the north had taken a long crowded bus ride to get to the ferry to cross the channel home.

He was tired of not understanding what everyone was saying. His French was not bad but he had to have them speak slowly so he could understand them. He wondered if he was making a mistake by taking a year for the apprenticeship in another country.

He would reconsider and see what might be done in England. He did remember South Hampton was filled with boat makers and maybe could do the same thing there. Anyway he was tired from travel and would decide later what to do.

The walk from the village dock across the beach he looked up to see the Brooker's cottage light was on and could see the flicker from the fireplace letting him know the sisters were home.

He took a deep breath and got a grip on the suitcase handle and walked briskly up the long steps to their home.

He knocked on the door trying to remain calm as he waited for someone to open the door.

"Matt, what are you doing here?" Cinny asked the tired traveler.

"I'm a door to door salesman, can't you tell?" He said sarcastically.

"Sorry, come in and sit down I will get Annie."

He sat down in front of the crackling fire with his case by his side on the floor.

"Oh, Annie, he's asleep, he looked exhausted when I opened the door."

"Let's get him upstairs to the spare bedroom."

They tried to awaken him and did long enough to have him walk up the stairs holding on to them with his arms around their shoulders.

They got him through the door and he fell on the high feather bed while they pulled his legs around to fit the bed and put the coverlet over him and left the cool room so he could sleep.

He awoke the next morning with the warm sun resting on his unshaven face.

He rubbed his eyes and looked around and couldn't remember where he was. After looking around the perfectly decorated room with white chintz bed and curtains that contrasted with the dark rich mahogany four poster bed with matching dresser and dressing table with three sided mirror.

He smiled when he remembered where he actually was and dimly remembered knocking on the door.

He heard a soft tap on the door and slowly opened it to see the love of his life looking up at him with soft blue eyes and her beautiful smile, the smile that melted and rendered him completely wordless.

"Are you all right?" She asked bringing a breakfast try and sitting it on the dresser.

"Yes, yes, just half asleep."

"I'll let you eat and take a shower, see you when you come down stairs."

He sat on the soft bed trying to wake up and get in control of himself.

He would eat first then take a shower as she had just suggested. The faint fragrance of her still remained in the room.

He had no idea what he was going to say to her to get her to change his mind about marrying him. All he knew he was not going to take no for an answer.

He hummed as he finished dressing and brushed his hair trying to dry it as much as possible.

Inching his way down the stair case he looked around to see where Annie was so he could start the dreaded conversation about their future hopefully together.

"Matt. Are you all right?"

He jumped at the sudden noise.

"I'm sorry I didn't mean to scare you."

"You didn't scare me; it was just so quiet…"

"I know, come let's go into the kitchen and sit at the table, everyone is gone so we will have some time together. We have some things to straighten out, don't we"?"

"Do we." He almost yelled as he dutifully followed her to the bright yellow kitchen.

"Would you like some tea?"

"Yes, please." He said sitting down and starting the dialog he came there for.

"I don't want to prolong the marriage conversation. I came here to tell you I put you in a very complicated situation by pushing marriage on you. Forcing my will on you by trying to manipulate your answer to what I wanted. I have had time to think about this whole thing. First of all I have loved you ever since I can remember. It was a natural instinct to ask you to marry me when I did. I neglected to take your side of our situation. I didn't allow you to get to know me, to romance you the way you deserved to have the chance to go through. All I could think of was me. All I could think of was fulfilling my dream. I did not once consider you and that you did not have the same dream I had for so many years. As a matter of fact you spent most of your life trying to get rid of me.

I finally came to this clear picture after a few dreams and many conversations with the old Frenchman, speaking slowly of course which allowed me to comprehend the full picture of our differing perception of our life and how we felt about each other, me, completely in love with you. You, not thinking about me at all with the exception of the times I was a pest."

"I am impressed with you Matt. That is so perceptive of you. You have the right idea, I never thought about you ever other than a 'pesky' little brother that my friends teased me about. You never gave me a chance to get acquainted when you returned home. I have had this time to think about us as well. I was too impatient with you and should have, since I am an older woman, taken the time to know you."

She smiled acknowledging she was older verbally and with acceptance of their age difference.

Annie got up to get them some tea when Matt stood up intercepting the tea.

"I want to do anything you want to do about our relationship. I will do what you say. I will romance you, bring you flowers, we will run on the beach like we did when we were growing up and go to movies that will make you cry and I can bring handkerchiefs for you to use. I want to hold your hand in church and let everyone see you are mine…that is if and when you say so." He said holding her tightly not wanting to look her in the face while he poured his heart out to her.

Stepping back and looking up at him for the first time really trying to pierce his soul to make sure he was sincere.

"Annie, you know I am completely in earnest when I tell you all of this you can surely feel what I am saying is true. You know I have loved you all my life, ever since I can remember you have been in my dreams. Where I went wrong was not allowing you time to get acquainted and know each other. I was only considering my side of the coin, and didn't even think about I was never in your life other than the fact I was a thorn in your side. All I want to ask you now is will you give me the chance to have a relationship with you and hopefully will end in marriage?"

The silence fell on the glowing room but this silence was not a dark one but an enlightening one they both were now aware of the difference of perception they each had of the other.

"I will, but you have to allow me to call you 'Mattie' once in a while." Anise smiled.

"Of course, and remember what happens each time you do." He winked.

"That sounds fair, Mattie."

He brought her close and this time softly kissed her sending her a silent message he loved her no matter what she called him.

CHAPTER THIRTY TWO

The sun was slipping below the horizon giving Ivy the signal it was time for her to lock up the shop and meet Les and Nigel at the empty town hall.

She had not wanted to go through this painful ordeal of overcoming her stage fright but with persistence from Collin and Tully she decided to at least try and see what would happen and how she would feel.

Les rolled the small stage to the wall at the back of the town hall slowly grateful it was easy to roll alone. He would be able to attach it to the wall securing it for solid safety for the ones on stage.

This had been designed the locksmith in the village and was used for the church choir and others when they had their Christmas Pageants, Easter Pageants and other community uses.

He was uneasy as he looked around to see if Nigel was there or coming through the door.

Les was not convinced his friend was sincere about completely taking alcohol out of his life as Les had been. Then again Nigel hadn't had the terrifying experience flying down the street to the church on a wobbly ladder on wheels and pledged to God that if he lived he would stop drinking.

It had been as simple as that for him as he knew he could never go back on his word and oath he promised his maker.

"Ivy, I am just securing the stage for you. We don't want you to sail away." He laughed.

"That is not very reassuring; hope you are only being funny. I don't know why I am doing this. I am not a professional singer."

"Hello, are we ready for this debut?" Tully asked putting his arm around her shoulders.

"No, I am not and I am starting to lose my breath. I don't know if I can do this…"

"I will stand beside you if you want."

"I will try that with you beside me, where is Colin?"

"He had some more paperwork for medical school and will be here shortly and I think Cinny is coming too."

"Oh, great, why didn't you invite the whole village?"

"I can, wait and I'll be right back." He laughed pretending to leave.

"No, stay here don't move or I will run."

"Where is Nigel?" Ivy asked.

"I don't know he was supposed to meet me here before you got here so we could set the stage for you. Hope he is all right."

"Me too, I am concerned he is not serious about his drinking."

"Hi, sorry we are late is it all right if Cinny is here?" Collin asked his sister.

"Yes, it is all right. Let's get this over with, I don't want to take all night, come on Costello."

"I'm with you Abbott." Tully laughed at her joke about the comedy team.

Ivy sat the guitar case on the lone chair on the empty stage as Les turned all the lights out except for the stage.

She took a deep breath sat the case on the floor, sat in the chair while Tully stood beside her.

Les brought another chair for him to sit in and try to make Ivy as comfortable as possible.

The lone pair on the stage looked as though they could spring up and run at any moment and run for their lives.

"Relax my love, take a deep breath Tully said arranging his chair to half face her but not cover her so the audience would be able to see her lovely face.

She started to play the guitar with the introduction of the song she would eventually sing when she could find the control of her voice.

Her hands shook as she played the old familiar song she had sung for the past few years filled with tears for the death of her husband and mother.

"Look out in the darkness, pretend there is no one there, only you and I here on the stage."

"I will try…" She said breathing deep once again and started to play once more.

The empty old hall filled with the beautiful melody from the beautiful handmade guitar and closing her eyes started to sing pretending she was in the storage room where she would pour her heart out night after night through the years.

She sang the popular song … "Reflection"…reflecting on images of you in my mind and heart…my life with you…trying to sing away the pain…the emptiness…loneliness… without you."

Les, Collin and Cinny sitting in the dark were overcome with both sadness and joy from the surprising talent coming from Ivy that evening.

Collin took Cinny's hand looking at her with love in his glistening eyes faintly showing in the darkness.

When Ivy softly ended the song there was not one sound in the building.

There came sighs of relief as Les turned the lights back on and ran up the steps to the frightened young woman.

"Ivy, I had no idea you were so gifted. You have a wonderful talent. You have to sing this song at least this one, hopefully more on our celebration night. I will help you and if I can find…"

At that moment they heard singing coming from Nigel as he staggered into the building.

"Nigel, where have you been?"

"I…was…I…was…I forgot." He slurred.

"You are drunk, I thought you quit drinking."

"I did…I did…I just had two little … tiny …drinkies at the pub with the lads." He smiled trying to straighten himself up.

"Did the lads know you had stopped drinking because you have a problem when you drink you do scary things?"

"Scary things, scary things, I don't do scary things."

"We won't go into that now, but you have. You missed Ivy's performance."

"That's all right Les, we will walk him home, is he still staying with Ron and Olive?"

"Yes, he is, thank you for taking care of him for me, I want to make some plans with Ivy before you leave, hold on for a few minutes and we can all leave together."

"Ivy, will you be able to meet us here tomorrow night and practice again so you will feel more and more confidant?"

"Yes, I will, it wasn't as bad as I thought tonight, but I need Tully to be with me on stage. At least for now."

"Sure, you can have Tully with you all the time. See you tomorrow night."

The small group left the stage intact for the next practice for Ivy.

Nigel started to sing as they walked down the lamp post lit street.

"Nigel, Shhhh, be quiet you will wake everyone up" Tully said holding him up so he wouldn't fall.

"Shhhh, be quiet don't wake anyone up…" Nigel whispered putting his finger to his lips and stumbled as he talked.

"Careful, you'll fall." Collin said.

"Shhhh don't talk. You'll fall…" Nigel muttered ready to pass out.

"Hang on Nigel we are almost home." Tully said

"Hang on Nigel…" Nigel repeated.

Ron and Olive were home to take over the inebriated friend.

"The lights are on good let's get him through the door and get it over with.

"Ron, open the door, Nigel is drunk." Tully said getting their attention.

"Nigel, what have you been up to?" Ron asked.

"I was just having a small drink with the lads."

"Looks like you had more than just a small one. I'll take him; you can go home now, thank you for bringing him home." Ron smiled. "We will talk to you tomorrow." Tully said gratefully closing the door on one very drunk friend.

"Well, I was hoping this night wouldn't focus on me and sure enough Nigel took the spotlight off me, I will thank him sometime." Ivy laughed as they walked breathing a sigh of relief after making sure Nigel was safely at home.

CHAPTER THIRTY THREE

The rain streamed down the window as Marilee pulled the while lace curtain back to see if there were any breaks in the dark gray clouds.

"Mummie, what am I going to do? I have told all my friends to come here today so we can practice what we will do with the ice cream freezers for the celebration?"

"You could go into the barn and do it there."

"Oh, there would be so much work to do to, well you know, clean up before we could ever practice."

"I'm sorry but that is the only other place you can meet. It is up to you, you could postpone it for another day."

"I know, but I am bored and need something to do."

"Well then, you and Wes can go out right now and start cleaning and making a spot for your freezers." Irene smiled.

"Oh, all right, I'll get Wesley to help; do you think I could ask Robert, Ryan and Homer to help?"

"I don't see why not, I am sure since it is raining they are free."

"Wesley, come let's go get the boys to help us with the freezers and take them into the barn after we clean it up." Marilee said with her usual dramatic flair.

"I don't want to do that… it… stinks out there." He curled his nose.

"You big baby follow me and let's bring the burlap bags too."

The boys were busy cleaning their shed from the latest mishaps involving their fireworks experiment that went awry.

"Rob, Ry, are you here?" Marilee knocked on their door.

"Yes, come in." Rob said.

"We need your help with our ice cream freezer practice in the barn with our friends."

"We are busy now, we will try to help later not now you can start and we will come later on if we are able." He said flatly.

"You mean you won't come with us now?"

"No, Marilee you heard me we have to clean up here and have some things we have to catch up on. We will be out there as soon as we can. Start without us."

"Oh, all right, but come as soon as you can please?"

"We will try our best to get there as soon as possible."

Marilee and Wes carefully made their way to the barn holding the oversized black umbrella and sloshing through the mud with their large rubber boots on dreading the job ahead they would have to start themselves without anyone's help.

"Wes, bring out the shovels so we can start shoveling and I will dry our rain slickers and brolley on the rail.

"Marilee, I am telling you I don't want to do this...I will stay for a little while but not all day. This is your deal, not mine. Your friends will be here shortly and I am leaving, I can't stand the smell here. So whatever you have to do you better make it fast."

"All right, all right…I am moving as swiftly as I can. Help me so you can leave. If you just stand there crying like a big baby we will never get it done."

"I am not a baby, I don't have to like the barn, and dad said I didn't have to like it."

"What do you mean he said you don't have to like the barn?"

"I don't want to be a farmer, he said I didn't have to be one or even enjoy the barn. So there."

Wes said as he turned up his nose to find shovels and start the horrible job he hated.

"I didn't know you talk to dad that way. What do you want to do then when you grow up?"

"I want to be an astronomer." He said brightening.

"An astronomer, well fancy that. Is it because you got that long telescope from Uncle Rex?"

"Partly, he just knew I loved looking at the stars."

"I think that is wonderful, huh, just think my little brother is going to be a famous astronomer." She said proudly. "I don't know about famous, but a regular one."

He chuckled at her approval.

"Marilee, why are you going to all this trouble? We only have to take turns with the boring job of sitting on the dumb rough burlap bags on the freezers until the ice cream freezes."

"We have to be organized with this. I have to make sure we are all together and not off playing somewhere in the crowds that night. You know how some of the boys are, all they want to do is play hide and seek, jump out and scare people as they walk by and they will surely get lost on purpose that night. I want to keep watch on them and make them promise they will full fill their duties."

"Oh, yeah right, they will promise to do their duties, according to us our duties are having fun and staying away from the girls, that is our sworn duty."

"Are you serious?"

"Of course I am serious, we can't stand to be around you girls, we want to run every time we see you. All you want to do is 'talk, talk, talk, chatter and then giggle about it all."

"Here is a shovel get started." Marilee said pushing the wooden handle into his hands.

"Where?"

"Over there." She said pointing to the stalls.

The pair started to shovel slowly grunting and moaning about the disgusting chore they elected to do.

"I'm tired, I need a rest."

Wes said propping his shovel on the wall.

"No, not yet we have lots to do before everyone gets here."

Marilee threw her hair back out of her face catching it on a long nail that held the horse's reigns which suddenly caught her off balance and she slid down to the floor she was cleaning.

"Are you all right, sis?"

Wesley asked standing over her smiling at her surprised fall.

"I have an idea, let's wait and we can all do this together and then everyone can enjoy this mess."

He laughed still looking down at her.

"Wes, get busy, I mean it." Marilee said flicking some manure on his face.

"You get busy." He said returning the same mixture to her face.

"You do as I say, mum said for you to help me."

She yelled at him raising her head off the floor and trying to stand up but slid back down again and getting angrier as she grabbed his leg and he fell down beside her.

"This is war Marilee." Wesley cried out rolling over away from her and picking up a larger moist cluster of manure and hay.

"Ouch, that hurts Wesley. You asked for it." Marilee screamed at her brother scratching through the droppings on the floor for the worst and largest piece she could rub on him as they continued roll on the greasy manure floor...

The siblings continued to scream and yell and tried to stand up but would fall back down as they pulled on each other not letting the other up off the barn floor collecting more on themselves than they had shoveled.

Irene, Phil, and the boys heard the ruckus in the barn and ran to see what was happening.

Phil flung the double doors open and saw his two children on the floor covered with layers of the smelly waste from the animals.

"Marilee. Wesley. Stop this instant." Irene screamed at them.

"Mum, dad." They shouted as they tried to untangle themselves from each other's grasp.

The two children sat with their heads bent down as their parents looked at the pair in disgust.

"You are both filthy. I can barely see your eyes; you are totally covered with filth. I am ashamed of you. Why would you ever do this?"

"I don't know, we just got carried away."

Marilee said.

"Yeah, she made me do it. I told her I wanted to leave but she made me, it is her fault."

"Wes, please, she needed your help. It is as much your fault as hers. I don't care who started it you both are in trouble, go to the house and throw these filthy clothes in the tub in the mud room. Don't you dare go into the house until we hose you down outside. Now go." Phil yelled pointing to the house.

Irene and Phil waited until their children left and then started to laugh holding each other so they would not be heard by their children.

Rob, Ry and Homer just stood still watching the parents of the muck covered children as they tried to get themselves together so they could go to the house and hose them down.

"Boys, will you help us and start cleaning this mess?"

"Sure, this is very unusual, it is usually us that are leaving the shed to go clean up, not them." Ryan laughed.

We will send those two back to help we just want to get one layer off them and have them put clean clothes on."

"That's all right we were going to help them anyway, but we didn't think it would be this way." Rob laughed.

"Oh, Phil all those children are coming here to practice the ice cream freezers."

"I'll go to the road and stop them and tell them it is postponed for another day. Is that all right?"

Homer asked.

"You are marvelous, what would we ever do without you? In fact this is something we wanted to talk to you three about. We will at dinner discuss our future together." Phil said thoughtfully.

Marilee walked outside after cleaning up happy the ordeal was over.

The sun was coming out and she felt like a new person.

She looked at the shed where the guys were working and she skipped down the path to the door.

Opening it wide she sang, "Thank you, thank you dear brothers, thank you so much for helping Wes and I out of our situation."

Robert, Ryan and Homer looked up from their work smiling and started to laugh wondering what she was up to.

"What's going go Marilee?"

"I just wanted to thank you for coming to mine and Wesley's rescue today. Not only did you help us clean up that horrible mess in the barn but you saved me from having to face all my friends covered in manure. I want to fix your favorite meal, what would you like for dinner?"

"Roast beef and Yorkshire Pudding." They all three said in unison.

"You shall have Roast beef dinner, 'Yorkshire Pudding' and apple pie and ice cream for dessert, how does that sound?"

"It sounds fishy to me, Marilee, what are you up to?"

"Why would I ever be up to anything?"

She said throwing her hair back out of her face to look in their faces innocently.

"Please, tell us now before you leave this shed." Ryan said.

"Oh, all right, I need your help again. In the midst of the manure fight we lost our burlap bags for the ice cream freezers. Do you have any idea where I could find some? Mummie won't help me she said it was my problem not hers."

"I thought so; do we still get the Pot Roast?"

"Of course, tonight everything I just said, I need those bags for the kids when they come to practice."

"I think we can do that. But from now on don't lie, just come out with whatever you want then if it will cost you a meal then so be it, promise?"

"Yes, promise, I didn't think it would this easy."

"Remember Marilee, the truth is that easy." Robert winked.

"By the way Marilee, you and Wesley looked like our two Jack Russell Terriers rolling in the manure. It was very entertaining watching you both.

"Thanks a lot Ryan, I really needed that, will you ever let me forget that?"

"Probably not." All three boys cheerfully yelled.

"Well I don't think you are being gentleman."

She said turning her nose in the air wanting to defend herself.

"We are sorry 'princess smelly', we didn't mean to upset you, please forgive us." Rob bowed to her.

"I have never been so humiliated." She yelled. She shut the door trying not to slam it and ran up the path in a cloud of loathing with herself and Wesley and their fight replay from heir vocal audience.

She was thankful she had something to take her mind off herself disgust and the need to focus on the promised favorite dinner.

She threw the kitchen door open and saw her mother at the sink and then started to cry.

"Marilee, what is wrong?" Irene asked her distraught daughter.

"Oh, mummy, I am so embarrassed, the boys made such fun of me just now in their shed. They were not gentleman at all."

"What did they say and do?"

"They called me 'Princess Smelly' and Wesley and I were rolling in muck like their Jack Russell dogs do." She sobbed on her mother's shoulder.

"Now, now Marilee, they were just trying to be funny, you know how boys are.

"I have never been so embarrassed I will not ever speak to them again."

"Marilee, listen just because your pride has been damaged don't do something to make things worse for you and Wesley and the bad situation that happened today. Just forget about it and hold your pretty little head up and ignore any other remark they might say. Show them how mature you are and then it will make them look like little school boys."

"Really, mummy, is it that simple?"

"Yes, I promise you if you let it so, don't ever say anything about it again it will go away and soon."

"I will try; I will try and thank you so much for helping me and listening to me." She said hugging her mother and praying she was right.

CHAPTER THIRTY FOUR

The indigo sky paraded the stars consortium in clusters and with others scattered throughout the massive extension of God's celestial theater.

The nightly show was never the same. The audiences could never complain they were bored with the extraterrestrial performances unique from night to night.

Cinny rested her head on the green winged back chair by the large paned bay window staring up at the evening splendor.

Taking a deep breath she decided it was time to start the overwhelming task of planning her wedding. She and Collin decided to be married before the celebration since Hazel was not able to set the exact date it would be held for things were not coming together smoothly in some of the committees.

They had begun the meetings with the vicar and the marriage instructions that were normal before couples could be married by him.

Cinny and Collin found they enjoyed the first one and were taught several things they had never thought about.

Richard softly brought out how important it was for them to keep in mind the success of a happy marriage and to make sure the other one was happy and to do whatever it took to keep it that way for the rest of their lives.

He carefully shared with them how he and Hazel were so different yet they made it work. He allowed her to be herself and do what she wanted to do to be free live her life fully. She allowed him the same privilege.

She twirled her red curls thinking about how she wanted to fix her hair.

"Cinny, are you awake?" Annie asked stoking the fire.

"Oh, you startled me. Yes, just thinking about the plans for the wedding. We are ready to set the date and are not going to wait for the celebration Hazel can't put it on the calendar until some of the problems are resolved in the committees."

"I will do whatever you want little sis, I think we should have the reception in the town hall to have the room to have for everyone in the village, don't you?"

"I never thought about that, but yes, we could decorate and make it nice for the reception. I will need you by my side and by the way will you be my maid of honor?"

"Yes…I would be honored." She laughed.

"I was thinking I want pink for your dresses and pink flowers, pink decorations. What do you think about that?" Cinny asked. "Well, I like pink and you like pink I guess pink it is then."

"You sound a little down. What is going on with you?"

"I always considered Matt an annoying little boy while at the same time I was unaware of it, he loved me and that was why he chased me all those years. I had no idea he actually had feelings for me. I only perceived this boy that was always there bothering me and my friends making fun of me for his attention.

Isn't life full of surprises and what is right under your nose but you can't or don't see what is happening around you."

"You have never been so philosophical what brought this on?

"Matt might have a change of heart about me, I mean our ages."

"What did he say to make you think that?"

"He called me an older woman and maybe he was too young for me." She started to cry remembering his words.

"He said what?"

"You heard me, he called me an older woman and that he might be too young for me." She cried again.

"Annie, I think he was having some fun. Think about it, does that sound like him?"

"No, that is why it hurt."

"Well, you have to admit you are the one always pointing out your age difference, he never has before, maybe he decided to face it and accept it make light of it."

"That was not pleasant to hear him talk like that."

"Talk to him and see what is going on and sort it out, don't feel sorry for yourself, do something about it like you always tell me."

"You are right, I will, I'll phone him later today when I get some time."

The sisters drank their chocolate, ate their biscuits, and with keeping their promise to each other of at least one laugh a day laughed at some of the more outrageous things from their past.

Matt locked the door to the antiques shop and looked up at the dark sky that suddenly brought back frightening memories of taking off into the night in France and flying to Germany to bomb the enemy and in the end liberate their ally.

Taking a deep breath he softly whistled as he sauntered down the dimly lit street to the Jarvis Chemist shop and grateful he was home, even though things were not going well with Anise Brooker.

The light was still on in the pharmacy so he opened the door and walked in looking around for Collin.

"Hey, ole' man where are you?"

"Up here on the ladder." Collin said carefully stepping down each step.

"What are you doing here?"

"I thought if you were free we could have some fish and chips, I'm hungry. Where is Cinny, I hardly see you without her you are like matching book ends." He scowled.

"You're in a mood tonight, where is your book end?"

"I don't know, I had to work late trying to organize things for the boys. I talked to dad and he won't come back, he still can't face it here without mum. I don't blame him, they were close. I understand part of what he is going through. He knows I want to leave and he just said have the boys take over and that he trusted Jeremy and the others. So that's what I'm going to do."

"My father has the same problem, he won't come back either, we both have had these shops dropped on us, but suppose it could be worse. At least we had something to come home to.

I thought you changed your mind about France. What about Plymouth or South Hampton, have you checked there?"

"Not yet but I am going to and wanted Annie to go with me. Speaking of her and Cinny, I just had a great idea, let's go see if they will fix our dinner?"

"You don't think it's too late?"

"Why not? They need to be spontaneous let's bring fish and chips, then they won't have to cook that might be better."

All right, that sounds good, let me lock up and I am ready."

The two friends talked their way up the hill to the Brooker cottage thinking about their surprise visit.

They reached the cottage and peered through the window where the light was on and could see the girls by the fireplace.

Annie caught the glint of Matt's blonde hair in the moonlight and started to scream and ran into the kitchen with Cinny behind her.

"Annie, what is wrong?"

"I just saw something outside the window. Be quiet." She said in the dark room.

"Matt, did you hear that?"

"Yes, I did, what was it?"

"I don't know it sounded like someone screaming."

"Let's see if the girls are all right." Matt said opening the kitchen door.

Suddenly Annie grabbed a pan and hit the unsuspecting intruder over the head.

"Get out of here, now, leave now and I won't hurt you." Annie yelled continuing to hit Matt with the pan.

"Annie, it's me, it's me." Matt yelled trying to wrestle the pan out of her strong grasp.

"Oh, no, Matt, Collin, what are you doing scaring us to death like that, are you all right by the way?" Annie laughed looking at the two young men surprised at the sudden attack.

"We just wanted to bring fish and chips for dinner. We didn't intend to frighten you. Sorry, but, Annie you are strong. You could have been a boxer." Matt said smoothing down his hair trying to make light of the altercation.

"Collin you have to promise you won't tell anyone that Matt was beaten up by a girl." Cinny chuckled.

"No, not a word…except…maybe one." Collin started to laugh as he continued.

Matt you should have seen yourself holding your hands over your head and ears trying get out of the reach of Annie and her frying pan." That was the funniest thing I have ever seen. She is strong." He stopped talking and bent over to catch his breath.

They all laughed at the picture of the tall young man trying to protect himself from the sudden attack from the love of his life.

"You mean for an older woman?" Annie asked sarcastically.

The two friends looked startled at each other.

"Maybe you are too young for me Matt. I am really not hungry; I am tired and I am going upstairs. Goodnight." She said taking off her apron throwing it on the table as she left the surprised guests and sister.

"What is wrong with her?" Matt asked.

"She told me about your comments on the phone yesterday about maybe you were too young for her and that she was an older woman."

"I meant it, I am tired of these silly games of me being too young for her. Enough is enough.

Well this has been an enjoyable evening but we have to go. See you tomorrow." Matt said grabbing Collin by the arm and ushering him out the back door…

"Well, that was interesting, guess I will have tea and go to bed." Cinny thought as she put the kettle on.

The two young men walked slowly down the hill with a completely different feeling than when they walked up to the cottage.

"I can honestly say that was not a great idea, surprising them." Matt said.

"Annie has grit." Collin sighed.

"Yep she has grit." Matt sighed.

"Not only grit…but a strong grasp of a frying pan as well, yes mate you have one with grit now if she will forget tonight and quit laughing at you. It is going to take a lot of grit on your part to with stand all her jabs as she brings it up from time to time. Sorry about the pun, jab not only her pan jabs but…" Collin laughed as he told his friend goodnight and left him standing alone out on the sidewalk with a look of wonder on his face.

Trying to regain his composure Matt whistled his favorite song as he walked home, recuperating from the episode that had just left him with bruises on his face and ears and hoped tomorrow would be a better day. He was going to South Hampton and find the boat builder he wanted to be apprentice to and fulfill his heart's desire.

CHAPTER THIRTY FIVE

The aroma of cinnamon buns fresh from the oven, and the sun streaming through the freshly washed yellow curtained window allowed a gentle breeze in from the Channel, still was not enough to cheer up the sisters as they silently washed dishes standing side by side.

"Do you suppose we should find the guys and see how they are?" Annie asked.

"I don't know, laughing at Matt really wasn't very nice now that I think about it. I was enjoying the moment so much I got carried away." Annie sighed remembering how funny Matt looked trying to protect himself from her attacks.

"Yes, he looked like a little boy caught coming home from school after being in a fight with a big bully. I am taking him some fresh buns to his shop, want to go with me?"

"Yes, let's take some buns, you take some to Collin and I'll stop by the antiques shop with Matt's"

"Let's hurry, I want to have lunch with him, so let's have the girls cover for us this afternoon and close as well."

"Yes, I agree, I am ready to face him after I beat him up last night. You said for me to find out if he has a sense of humor, now I will find out." Annie laughed.

The sisters put the bakery baskets filled with buns and cakes for the intruders into their bicycle wicker baskets.

They pedaled slowly yet each wanted to hurry but held their speed to a minimum not to appear too anxious.

"See you Annie, good luck." Cinny waved good bye as they approached Matt's shop on the corner.

"Meet you at home tonight, good luck. Tell Collin hello."

"I will, so long."

Annie parked the bicycle in the back of the shop and knocked softly on the back door as she carefully smoothed the burgundy napkins she had made for the tea shop that wrapped the heartfelt offering.

"Annie, won't you come in." Matt smiled grateful to see her.

"Thank you, here are some fresh buns, I just wanted to say hello." She said clearing her dry throat.

"Thank you it smells wonderful, let me put them in a covered dish so they won't dry out. Come with me."

She followed him to the small office he had in the back room.

"Matt, I…I…need to apologize for last night. I am so sorry for the way I …well beat you up."

"I know, we frightened you and we are so sorry, but in the end you got the best of the situation." He laughed finally able to not take himself so seriously.

"I know, so let's call us even and forget about it. Let me see the damage. Oh, not too bad, just a little bruise there."

She said looking up at him touching his cheek.

I will," He said as he took her hand and looked into her eyes.

"Yes, I do know how strong you are, Mattie."

She half smiled.

He took her in his arms with the cue from her that all was well because she said the magic word Mattie and this time he didn't ignore it as he held her close.

"I want to have some fun, we have had 'stiff upper lips' too long and now it is time we just enjoy, well I will try to enjoy mine, it is stiff you know or I would kiss you." He laughed.

"Oh, I am sorry, I promise I will never hit you again, but I can't promise I won't tease you about it from time to time." She laughed.

"I knew that was coming, Collin said I will have to prepare to face this in the future.

Now, what are you doing the rest of the day?"

"Cinny and I asked Polly and the girls to take over for us and close up as well."

"Great, how would you like to take a trip to South Hampton with me? I want to discuss something with you. We could have lunch on the way and dinner there before we come home?"

"That sounds wonderful let me tell Cinny and then I need to go home and change, will you meet me at the cottage and pick me up there?"

"I will be very happy to do that." He clicked his heels as he bowed down to tenderly and lightly kiss her hand with his bruised lips.

The road to South Hampton from the village was much more narrow and winding than Matt had remembered. It had been years since he had driven in England. The old family truck that had been used by his father ever since he could remember was difficult to maneuver unless he kept the speed at a low rate.

"Sorry we can't go faster but this old truck won't go fast and besides it's a beautiful day and I am in beautiful company and the coast is outstanding. What a lucky man I am."

"You are a lucky man, you returned home safe and sound."

"What was it you wanted to talk to me about?"

"I have changed my mind about taking the boat apprentice in France. There are too many things I need to do here, you being the first on the list of things I need to take care of. I wanted to talk to some guys I became acquainted with in the RAF that live there. They know some of the boat builders that live close to them. There are many old ship builders there. Surly someone needs an apprentice willing to work hard.

"That would be a good idea, then would you drive back and forth then from there each day?"

"I don't know for sure, I might work it out to do the apprenticeship two days a week and stay home the rest of the week to keep an eye on you and the shop. My father will not now or later come home he lives not far from there and that is what I wanted to talk to you about to help me sort through and make the best plan for us all."

. I am glad you want to please us all and that is a wonderful sweet thing for you to do, all I am saying is that in the end you have to make the decision to allow you to follow your dream. My mother and father always told us that, I just haven't had a dream to follow. Cinny and I were caught in the middle of a war without parents and two businesses to keep open."

"You don't have a dream at all, not even a small one?"

"Not really, just to do the things I need to do to keep the doors open and try to do better tomorrow what I fell short of today."

"I am glad we have this day together, we haven't had a chance to be together alone, this is nice." He smiled

"Now, when are we going to eat, I am ravenous."

She smiled back at him looking at his bruised face.

CHAPTER THIRTY SIX

Les finished unpacking the shirts he had ordered to fill his emptying shelves. Peacetime was setting in but his orders hadn't arrived any sooner than before to his dismay.

He decided to order as much as they would allow him to and then hope for the best.

He completely and thoroughly cleaned his shop discarding everything he had needed to get rid of for years that he had collected and since he was no longer drinking he could see more clearly junk that he had shoved into the bulging storage room.

With Hazel's help he gave the unwanted items to the church bazaar that was trying to make money for the village celebration.

Feeling good about his promise to God that he would stop his decades of alcohol if his life were spared, he felt the future was bright.

A very surprising event had happened; the old cupid's arrow had struck and found him looking forward to the evenings after closing the store which in the past he would dread. The loneliness of the dark nights with no lights allowed to shine anywhere outside and only very dim ones inside.

He knew Daphne Shaw only vaguely and never for a moment ever thought about a relationship with the twenty year difference in their ages.

He did however think she was attractive and enjoyed talking to her from time to time.

Now he spent his days looking forward to closing time so they could have dinner together whether dinning out or each one would take turns cooking.

He found food tasted better now and he thoroughly liked shopping each day for meals whether with her or alone.

His thoughts that morning were becoming clearer of Nigel's inability to quit drinking. He was trying to think of a way to help his old friend so he could enjoy life as much as he was with no morning after headaches.

He decided to phone him at the Simon's and invite him to have dinner with them that evening.

"Olive, is Nigel there?"

"Yes, he is…he slept in the back room…I'll get him for you."

"Nigel, Les for you on the phone." She called through the closed door.

"I will call him back." He said rubbing his temples.

"Les, he'll call you back, he isn't feeling too well, sorry."

"Thank you Olive I'll be over in a bit. Keep him there until I come." "I will."

Les locked the shop and walked down to the Simon's grocery...

"Hi, how are you this beautiful morning?"

She asked admiring his immaculate attire and graying hair that added to his handsome aging face.

"I am doing very well, Olive you are looking well this morning. I like the haircut, you look very glamorous. So Nigel just won't stop drinking then?"

"No, we have not had any success at all. I think it is time we get Hazel to help him the way she helped you. But I do understand you made a promise but she did help didn't she?"

"Yes, she was there when I needed someone to talk to and I did pour out my weary drinking soul many days."

"I am going to see her today, do you have any ideas?"

"No, I have tried to get him to accept there will come a day or night he will wish he had not taken a drink. There would come a time something bad will happen, just a question of when as it was with me. He won't listen."

"He was sleeping in the back yard until Ron heard him moaning early this morning. We thought something bad had happened. He just passed out though."

"I think, if you don't mind I will walk him down to the vicarage."

"We don't mind at all, we are tired of trying to keep him from destroying himself. In fact we were going to ask him to leave today. Will you tell him for us?"

"Yes, I will tell him, he can stay with me for a while, I need to step up and help him more than I have been. She and I… well." He stopped.

"I know you are having dinner together and I think that is wonderful, you both deserve to be happy and enjoy life together."

"Olive, do you think she is too young for me?"

"No, Les, not at all, she looks older…I don't mean in a bad way and you look younger which is a good thing." She laughed.

"Thank you, now, have you heard anyone making fun of us?"

"No, not at all, if you want the truth everyone is happy about your new friendship."

"Good, that makes me feel better, I was afraid I was the village joke."

"No, you are not a joke, you can relax. Now take Nigel to Hazel so we can try to save his life." She laughed.

"Nigel, are you awake?" He called.

"I am, come in."

"What do you want so early?"

"I want you to go for a walk with me to the vicarage and talk to Richard and Hazel. I am worried about you old man and I don't want to lose you."

"Let me take a shower and I will go with you, come with me to the house I need to take a headache tablet."

"Let's go old man, and get the start of a new life for you."

The two old friends left the shop to let Nigel take a very hot shower for the impending visit with Hazel to start hopefully a new lease on his very shaky life.

Combing his thinning gray hair with trembling hands and straightening his Sunday tie, He was trying to look better than he felt Nigel silently tried to prepare himself for the impending meeting with his friends.

"We better get going down the hill, they are waiting for us." He said ushering Nigel out the door.

"Les, how have you completely quit drinking, you haven't had one drink?"

"I told you Nigel, I promised God if he spared my life I would stop, he did and I have kept my promise I have not had one drink since that day on that wild ladder ride to the church yard."

"I have promised many times that I wouldn't drink again, but something happens and I can't help myself. I start to feel alone and weak without that drink. It seems to give me confidence and I overcome that frightening feeling when I drink."

"I know that scary feeling, I had to do a lot of self-talk, I remember one night I was locking up the shop and feeling really weak, tired and alone. I had the thought, 'a large glass of ale would taste so good and would make me feel better. Then the promise I made seemed to glow in my mind on a bill board and I saw the words, 'I promised God I will never drink again.' It was incredible. It was like a moving picture in my head. I have the feeling God does know when I need Him the most and comes to my rescue. Nigel, Hazel, the vicar and I are going to help you with this new life being free of these chains that are weighing you down. We are going to be there for you to get through this and hopefully you will be able to promise yourself that you will stop drinking and enjoy this wonderful world God has given us. We can do this together, Nigel, but in the end it is up to you, we can't do it for you, only offer our care and concern while you get in control of this bad and self-destroying habit."

"You should be a vicar Les, and I agree I am the one that has to do this, it is true I can't do it alone."

"You will never be alone, I promise. I may not be able to be at your total beck and call, but I will as much as possible. You have my word on that."

"Thank you, let's go, I want to get this over with, I mean, started." He smiled at his slip of the dread he felt of the beginning of this new and uncertain life with his old friend alcohol.

CHAPTER THIRTY SEVEN

The Brooker's Tea Shop was empty with the breakfast customers well on their way filled with the tasty fare prepared and served by the young owners.

Hazel always loved to walk into the shop and have the aroma of freshly baked goods fill her senses with the goodness life had to offer from the enjoyment of these simple pleasures.

"Hazel, please sit down and we will bring tea and what would you like this morning to go with it?" Annie asked seating her friend at the window overlooking the channel.

"I would love a hot cinnamon bun. I have an idea I would like to talk to you and Cinny about when you have a moment."

"Sure, I will bring your tea and bun and have Cinny join us, it won't take long, she is helping clean the kitchen."

"Cinny, please hurry, Hazel is here and would like to talk to us about something can you let Polly take over?"

"Yes, she is outside clearing the tables, I'll talk to her, by the way, she said to tell you thank you for the raise in her salary. She was so excited you would have thought she just became rich."

"She deserves a lot more but in time she will get more, what would we do without her?"

"I know, I don't know what we would do, now without her and her friends especially since I will be moving with Collin to Oxford this fall quarter. You know he was accepted last week for the medical program?"

"Yes, you told me and I am so happy for you both, I just don't want to think about not having my little sister here with me, and what am I going to do without you?"

"Now, Annie, you have Matt, remember the tall blonde handsome guy that makes you laugh?"

"I know, thank goodness I do or I would have to move to Oxford too." Annie laughed.

"I will bring a pot of tea in a minute go and sit with Hazel."

"Well, Annie, I would imagine you will be lonely without your little sister here with you. Hope you won't miss her too much." Hazel said.

"I will miss her, she was part of me all my life, I don't want to think about it too much now, and I will do the best I can when that day comes."

"Cinny, here you are, I have an idea for you and Collin to think about. I was told you wanted to get married before the celebration because it wasn't on the calendar yet and that is why I am here to let you know after talking to each chairman we have set the date for the 25th of June at 7:00 P.M."

"That is a precise date, and time, it sounds good to me that will give us about three weeks to prepare our orders and give Polly and her friend's time to organize. They will be doing most of the hard work." Annie said.

"That should work." Cinny added.

"Now, the idea I had, Cinny, is to ask you and Collin if you would like to get married at 6:00 P.M. and have your reception at the celebration. I was thinking since the whole village will be at your wedding why not combine that and the celebration so we can really celebrate?"

The sisters looked at each other and laughed.

"What is so funny?" Hazel asked.

"We were wondering too that since everyone will be getting ready for the village night that might take away from my wedding attendance and reception." Cinny said.

"That is a wonderful idea Hazel; you are the most incredible person I know for good ideas and working out problems. What would our village do without you?"

"Well, I know some of our neighbors might not agree with you." She laughed thinking about Nigel and Les.

"That makes me feel so good and I can't wait to tell Collin we were just talking about this last night. I will go now and tell him and let you know what he says, Hazel. Pardon me for leaving. Talk to you later today about it." Cinny said as she rushed out throwing her apron on the counter.

She climbed on her bicycle and flew down the hill to the chemist shop.

Collin was filling a prescription as he looked up and saw Cinny standing in front of him with a big smile on her pretty flushed face.

"What are you doing here, my love?"

Trying to get her breath she said. "Hazel had the most wonderful idea about our wedding and reception. Hurry and come to the back office with me I have to tell you all about it." Cinny said.

"I will be there in a minute, so go on back, Ivy may be there, but she will give us privacy."

"No bother, she can hear what I have to say, hurry." She said rushing to the back room.

"Cinny, what are you doing her so early in the day?"

"I have something to talk to Collin about our wedding. Please stay and you can hear the plan as well. By the way how are you and Tully getting along?"

"Oh, fine, we are just good friends and are enjoying doing things together. I am helping him with his dogs for the talent show at the celebration. It is very interesting how he teaches them and what he actually wants the audience to see. I have never been around animals and this has been quite an adventure for me and I am enjoying watching him with them."

"I hear he is very serious about you Ivy. I am sorry if I sound too nosey, but I think you make a wonderful couple and can see you in a more permanent relationship, such as marriage." Cinny smiled at her future sister-in-law.

"Please, don't say any more about this, I don't know how to handle talk like that. All I know is for now we enjoy each other's company and that is all." Ivy said closing the subject.

"All right, my little one, what is this big idea you have?"

"Sit down and get comfortable, Hazel had the idea when she set the

'End of the War' celebration on the 25th of June at 7:00 P.M.….now, she wanted you and I to think about getting married on that day at 6"00 P.M. and have our reception at the celebration…what do you think about that?"

"Well, that would solve everything we just talked about last night wouldn't it?"

"Yes, we knew the whole village would want to be at our wedding but it was so close to the celebration isn't she wonderful to think about that?"

"That is a wonderful idea; combine both celebrations in one event…." Ivy smiled.

"Collin, may I tell her it is all right with you?"

"Yes, and didn't you have something to ask Ivy?"

"Oh, yes, Ivy, will you please consider to be a bridesmaid?"

"How thoughtful, well, yes, I will be happy to be a bridesmaid, what color are you going to have our dresses?"

"Well, pink if it is all right with you. Annie said O.K."

"Just so it isn't green, "Ivy laughed.

"Thank you Ivy and I promise green won't even be on the fabric." Cinny said.

"I have to get back to work, see you tonight for dinner?"

"Yes, let's have dinner with Annie and Matt and Ivy and Tully?"

"That's fine with me will you set it up? It won't be long and we won't be able to be with them, we will all be going our separate ways."

"That's true, I didn't think about that I will to get us all together." Ivy said.

"See you tonight, let us know what time." Cinny said as she rushed out as swiftly as she came in wanting to hurry and tell Hazel the good news about them accepting her wonderful idea.

CHAPTER THIRTY EIGHT

Matt stepped back to look at his small model sail boat he had been working on to keep alive his dream of one day becoming a real boat builder and start his apprenticeship with the man he had recently met in South Hampton. He felt very confident about choosing him out of the several men in the area competent enough to teach him what he needed to know for his new vocation.

Changing his plans from France to England was the right decision he could feel. He knew Annie needed to be close to the Brooker's shops and he to his antique shop and this would solve everything.

Taking the quick trip to the southern shores of France when he abruptly left home in pursuit of fleeing the pain caused from his sudden marriage proposal to Annie and her cold refusal. This trip awoke in him just how unrealistic he had been with his sudden proposal to Annie. He had the chance to see how he had been in love with her ever since he could remember and she only knew him as the annoying boy around her every corner.

He was wondering if his future with Annie was going anywhere or if she was just trying to be polite because the answer was no.

"What are you so into that you didn't hear the doorbell as I walked in?" Collin asked.

"Oh, Collin, I was just finishing this sail boat model. What are you doing out of your pharmacy this time of day?"

"Well, I have some news, Cinny and I have actually set the date of our wedding and I wanted to ask you if you will be my best man?"

"Of course I will be your best man, when is the big day?"

"Well, Hazel made the suggestion that we get married the same day of the celebration only an hour earlier then we could have the combined reception and celebration at the same time on the 25th of June." He smiled.

"That is only three weeks away, are you ready for that my lad?"

"I know it is soon but I am ready and so is Cinny we just want to be man and wife and start our life together as soon as possible."

"Good for you, now, what are we wearing?"

"Black Tux's, is that all right with you?"

"Fine with me, we need to get to Les's shop and get it all sorted out."

"That is a good idea, I was thinking London, but Les will be better, he is a good tailor."

"I wish we could make it a double wedding, but we aren't there though." Matt sighed hopefully.

"By the way, Cinny and I, Ivy and Tully want you and Annie to come to dinner tonight, it won't be long and we will be separated so let's get together as much as we are able, can you call Annie and find out for me?"

"Sure, we were going to the movies so we will change to dinner with you all. I didn't think about us going our separate ways and will be a while before we will be able to see each other."

"Cinny brought it to my attention; I think she is going to have a hard time living away from her sister."

"I know Annie dreads her leaving the area. She tries not to talk about it but it keeps coming up. I just didn't put you and me in that same situation. I will miss you mate."

"I will you as well,"

"I better get back to work; Ivy is with a salesman and couldn't get tonight sorted out so I told her I would. See you at seven at the Beach Front?"

"That will be fine, see you later."

Matt cleaned his hands from the wood stain he used for his boat and began to feel the need to ask Annie once again to marry him.

'I wonder...I just wonder if...no, probably not.' He thought pushing the thought of proposing again this soon out of his mind. Taking the red velvet ring box out of his pocket he decided to put it in the shop's safe and forget about marriage.

He was beginning to feel it would not happen and not to get his hopes up again, he couldn't stand another rejection. He was going to relax and enjoy his new adventure in boat building and keep that his only focus for the future.

"Annie, may I pick you up at half past six this evening to meet Cinny,
Collin, Ivy and Tully at the Beach Front Café instead of the movies?"

"That sounds good to me, I would like that Mattie."

She smiled knowing he couldn't reply that name with a kiss over the phone.

"You are charming I must say for an older woman. Collin told me about the wedding and reception at the celebration. That is a great idea to combine it so they will get the attention they deserve. It will be great to see them dance under the paper moon."

"Uncle Reggie told me it was your idea, the paper moon, I mean and with the cardboard sea. He also said you were doing it for me."

"He did, did he?"

"He did, I think it was a very sweet gesture, I ruined your plans and put a dark cloud on your moon and sea, didn't I?"

"Well, in a way, but I can see now I was too presumptuous. I see now how one our relationship was one sided. Maybe I am too young for you. Sorry to put you through all that." He smiled eager to make her angry.

"Maybe so." She said curtly hanging up on his 'too young' statement.

'Ha...He thought I am going to do a turn around and rub it in about our ages to the point she will have to either marry me or end this suspense.'

The three couples sat at their favorite table by the large window that gave the panoramic view of the channel. The moonlight caught the smooth water's reflection and illuminated the beautiful scene of the English Channel to its ultimate beauty.

"Well, Collin, so you and Cinny will be leaving the night of the celebration?" Matt asked sitting with his arm around Annie's shoulder.

"Yes, we will leave when the reception is over and have danced at least one dance under your paper moon." Collin smiled and winked at Cinny.

"Matt, when are you leaving to start your apprenticeship in South Hampton?" Ivy asked.

"The day after the celebration, I have everything organized here with Jeremy and Adam and I wanted to thank you again Ivy for your help with them and keep me informed. It will be good to finally get started; it has been a long time in the making."

"Will you just stay there and come home once in a while or will you have set days there and home?" Collin asked.

"I am going to see how it goes, I'm not sure about a schedule I'll have to wait and find out how things go."

"How is your Uncle Reggie and Aunt Lily settling in, Annie?" Ivy asked.

"Quite well, they are in London now until they are able to leave permanently. It took longer than they thought. Hopefully at least by the celebration, the manager of their shop had to finish his job with his current employer after giving notice before he could take over for them. They will be back and forth several times before the move will totally be made complete. When you get into these sorts of things it always takes longer than at first expected." Annie smiled faintly at Matt.

"You have that right, what we want and what we get and how long it takes may take a lifetime." He said looking away from her.

Anise could feel a sudden chill from Matt.

'Wonder what set him off.' She thought searching his face for that wonderful smile, but it was not there.

"Tully, I heard your dog act for the talent show is wonderfully funny. Ivy said you have quite a gift as a dog trainer." Cinny said.

"Well, it is rewarding to be able to control a situation; life is not always controllable is it?"

"No, that's for sure." Matt agreed.

"Let's all promise we shall all get together at least once a month here in the village, we surely should be able to do that." Cinny said.

"I think that is a marvelous idea, if we plan it we should be able to, maybe not once a month but as often as we can." Collin said.

"Let's make a toast to that, since I am Collin's best man I shall toast to the future wedding of my best friend and his future bride." Matt said raising his water glass with the other friends to bring to pass all their hopes of a happy new life even with all the uncertainties involved.

Avoiding Matt's stare, Anise glanced away remembering his 'older woman' remark.

CHAPTER THIRTY NINE

Reggie put the canvas top down on his old pale yellow MG Roadster. The tan leather seats were still soft and comfortable. He took special care of it since he bought it with the money from his first large painting sale.

His aging body was not as agile as it used to be, he felt he would start a physical training routine to get in shape. He had let himself go working to fulfill all his art customers' orders.

"Now, Lily are you ready to start out for your new life on the coast?" He smiled helping her with her baggage and strapping the bags on the back of the small car with his.

He loved the way she dressed in loose casual pastel pants and tops. She was feminine with a touch of sophistication. Her smile was ingrained in his heart and soul. He never seemed to have the words to tell her how much she meant to him and how beautiful he thought she was. He tried to tell her silently with his tender loving care...

"I suppose, I hope this turns out well, I can't help but think how extreme this is at our age. Are we up to helping with the girls business? I am concerned I won't be able to satisfy Anise, she is quite precise in everything she does."

"I wouldn't be too concerned, she has lots of help from the youths that came from London and they wanted to stay there and work and live after the war. She must be easy to work for if they want to stay on. Don't you think? Besides, we aren't that old we are faintly fifty."

"Faintly fifty, you are delicate with our age, I've never heard it put that way before where did you get faintly fifty?"

"Oh I heard two old dears talking the other day in our shop and one said to the other 'My dear you are only faintly seventy.' I thought how we were only faintly fifty."

"That was sweet, you know you are getting softer as you get older, the crusty young artist that knew everything has turned into a soft older gentleman who is not afraid to admit he doesn't know it all. Yes, I do find that refreshing and that is why I am going along with this plan. I know you will be with me all the way and if I should any problems you will help me, won't you?

"Of course my love, I shall always be there for you." He smiled watching her graying brown hair blow in the wind.

Lily Dunsworth Brooker was a popular artist and had been inundated with work as well as her famous husband. She was tired of living in fear she would not be able to satisfy her clients and thought the break with helping her husband's nieces into a new life with Cinny going to live in Oxford with her soon to be husband would give her the break she needed. Her tired face proved she needed a change. Her classic features were still crisp and clean. Her ivory skin still supple didn't truly show her age. Her shimmering large blue eyes still lit up when her husband of twenty years would come through the door.

"Lily, do you get sad when you think about us not able to have children?"

"Are you sad about it?"

"I asked you first."

"Yes, I must admit there were times I had longed for children to take to the park and watch them play with their dog and then tucking them in at night. But in time the pictures faded and I accepted life as it was. I found with my art and my loving husband I was happy.
Why, do you still want children?"

"No, not now, I decided our life would be what we made it, children or not. I only knew I was so happy I had sense enough to marry you. We do have nieces we can get to know better."

"Spoken like a true gentleman that you are, do you fancy a cup of tea?"

"I do, let's stop in the next village and have one and spend the night."

"Yes, this is almost halfway, I don't enjoy driving like I used to."

"You sound like you are getting past faintly fifty." She smiled to let him know how much she did love him.

The couple sat silent each deep in their own thoughts feeling the change in the wind that blew on their faces and through their graying hair.

Lily smiled as she realized how much she did love her husband, how much she liked his saunter when he walked and moved his medium muscular frame when he moved articulately as he painted letting her know he was in control and everything was fine. Yes, she did love her gentle, kind husband and felt refreshed as they headed for a new part of their life in Brooker's Village-On-Sea.

CHAPTER FORTY

Anise awoke to the light tapping sound of rain pouring down her bedroom window. The grayness of the morning matched her mood. She couldn't shake the feeling she had lost Matt. His cold retorts from the night before were etched in her heart. He had made her feel old. She wasn't prepared for the turn in his countenance and his cool behavior and words still rang in her mind to his seemingly change of heart towards her.

She threw back the pink duvet and slid out of her large feather bed she had slept in all her life. Stretching up towards the white ceiling she felt her tired muscles resisting her effort to move.

'Come now old girl, you can't let me down now; we have a big day ahead. Uncle Reggie and Aunt Lily would be driving in that morning and meet at the Tea Shop for breakfast.

Oh, I need a tonic; a quick brisk walk on the beach would do before I take a shower. 'As she remembered walking in the rain with Matt just a few days ago she hurried down the old steps to her favorite place to go. Now things seemed so different so quickly. Her uneasy feelings hung over her as the gray clouds hung over the beach as she moved faster and tried to shake the dark feelings about Matt that lingered in her uneasy heart.

"Annie, where have you been?" Cinny asked her.

"I needed a walk before my shower, now I feel better and ready to see our Aunt and Uncle. Let's prepare a large English Breakfast for them, shall we?"

"Is that too much for them? They are not getting any younger you know."

"Cinny, they aren't that old. Don't make them into something they are not. Our Uncle Reggie and Auntie Lily are energetic, lively and fun."

"I didn't mean they were old exactly, just getting a little gray." She smiled at her sister now allowing her to put them into an early grave.

"We will make them a meal fit for the king and queen."

Anise began the large meal for her father's younger brother. She was grateful for them coming to live there in the small cottage so she wouldn't be alone after Cinny left in a few short weeks.

She continued to dispel the gloom from Matt's behavior the night before. Her impulse was always to stay busy and work hard and things would get better, but this time it wasn't working. She was beginning to feel concerned. Yes, it was a new experience and her old routine was not making this dark cloud go away.

"Uncle Reggie, Auntie Lily, we are so glad you are here." Anise said breathlessly finishing the table setting for them on the shady part of the patio dining area.

"Your teashop is lovely, we are so glad we can be here close to you, and get better acquainted. What smells so wonderful?" Reggie asked hugging his nieces.

"Are you ready for a full English Breakfast?

We have beans, bacon, sausage, tomatoes, potatoes and eggs with lots of fried bread, and pots of tea to have with sticky buns afterwards."

"Reggie, we will have to be carried away in an ambulance if we eat all that." Lily laughed.

"No, we won't we shall eat slowly and enjoy every bite as we catch up with the last few years." He said wrapping his arm around her shoulders.

"Well, only this one special day to start off our new life here in this beautiful village."

The four ate, talked, and laughed as they began their new life together.

"Annie, where is Matt, I thought he might be here to join us?"

"Working I suppose, he won't be here with us and is getting the shop ready to leave in the boys care while he is taking his apprenticeship in South Hampton. He will drive back and forth from time to time. His solid plan can't be made until he's there for a while and hasn't made a schedule but will soon. Then Annie will know when to expect him. Things are a little up in the air." Cinny chimed in.

"Let's get you both settled in your cottage, are you ready?"

"We're ready and I want to check the small building in the back and make it into our art studio. I know the cottage is great, we've stayed there for weekends when your parents were ….well, here."

He said looking down remembering how much he missed his brother.

CHAPTER FORTY ONE

Matt locked the door to the shop feeling empty and lonely. All his bright hopes for a future with Annie seemed out of sight. He couldn't see them together any longer and wasn't sure what had happened to change his positive attitude about sharing his life with her.

He was beginning to sense that this part of his future was not his first priority that his apprenticeship would take her place and she would be down the line. No more false hopes and misleading words from her would deter him this time. His focus was going stay on ship building.

Matt's soul searching through the years revealed to him that he was always too optimistic at first sight. He realized later in the war optimism had its place but life was not full of positive outcomes. He soon learned that he would have to take things as they came which was coming into view that evening.

He walked to Collin's shop determined to accept whatever happened and put things in their proper place.

The shop was empty ready to close the door. Collin finished his prescription refill and placed it in the paper bag ready for tomorrow's delivery.

"Hi ole man, do you and Cinny have plans tonight?"

"No, she and Annie are having a girl's night out. I am free, what's on your mind?"

"I thought we could play some pool and talk. I need to get this pressure released. I'll buy dinner at the Beach Front first."

"Sounds good to me I didn't have time for lunch today. Let me change my jacket and I am ready to roll." He laughed.

"What's on your mind tonight Matt?" Collin asked as they walked down the lamp lit street.

"It's Annie, I've decided to forget her and put my apprenticeship first forget any plans with her, I can't take her lack of seriousness about marrying me."

"What brought this on all of a sudden?"

"Things just add up to the fact she is not serious about me, I am only someone to laugh at. I never know what to expect from her, I can't stand the uncertainty anymore."

"That doesn't sound like my old positive buddy."

"I know, but she won't allow me into her thoughts for the future other than her aunt and uncle coming to live here to help her since Cinny is moving."

"Have you asked her to sit down and just talk about her feelings and thoughts about the future?"

"Well, no not exactly."

"Well then, why don't you just call her and have a quiet dinner and a long walk and talk."

"I will tomorrow, I suppose it is partly my fault. I was afraid she would tell me off forever."

"No, I think you are wrong about that and do call her tomorrow first thing. Now, let's go, I fancy some fish and chips."

The morning sun streamed through the antique shop's black paned windows spotlighting the recently varnished furniture Matt had redone to make them more saleable.

He reached for the phone to make the call he dreaded. Confrontation was not his strong point. He felt vulnerable and dreaded the call.

"Hello, Annie, Matt, are you free this evening?"

"Yes, I am, why?"

"I wanted to take you to dinner and go for a long walk and talk about our future and if there is one."

"Oh, all right, what time?"

"How about six o'clock?

"That will be fine, see you then." She said setting the phone in its cradle slowly thinking about what they would be talking about that evening.

The day flew by and it was ready to dress for the evening.

Annie couldn't decide what to wear. She was tired of all her clothes, rather lack of choices.

She threw on her old white terry robe drying off after her hot shower.

Peering into the round mirror in the remodeled pink and green bathroom she shook her hair out of the curlers she had put in earlier hoping it was dry.

'Good she thought. Hope it combs out right. I do look old. What am I doing even thinking about marrying a younger man than he will hate me in a couple of years?'

She moved slowly down the stairs still feeling old and tired.

The doorbell rang and Matt came through the door as Cinny let him in.

"You look great Annie."

"Thank you, so do you." She smiled softly wanting to change the subject.

"See you later Cinny." Anise said hugging her sister goodbye.

Matt drove his old truck slowly down the drive to the main road.

"You said you had something for us to talk about?" Annie asked.

"I don't know, I suppose so." He said dreading to bring up the subject.

"We don't have to talk about anything you don't want to talk about."

"You wouldn't want to anyway, let's just have a good evening meal and enjoy the peace and beauty." He said deciding not to bring up the subject of marriage again. He didn't seem to have the heart to go into that dark space without the light knowing he would come out happy with her decision.

CHAPTER FORTY TWO

The day dawned with the brightness of the sun turning the sky orange letting the inhabitants of Brooker's Village-On-Sea it would be a beautiful day for the wedding and celebration.

Marilee heard the faint tap on her door and knew it was her mum waking her up to help her start the long day.

"Marilee, Marilee, Marilee down the stream." Irene sang going into the bedroom wanting to keep her daughter in a good mood.

"Yes, mummy I am awake but I don't want to get up, may I just sleep in a bit longer?"

"No my little one you may not, we have tons of work to do so we can all enjoy our wonderful day. We even have the wedding at six when you can dress up in your flower girl dress. Are you excited about that?"

"I suppose so and it is a lovely dress you made for me."

"Thank you my dear, now up we come and get going breakfast is almost ready so get into your work clothes and we will take our bath later."

"I will be down in a minute."

"Will you please let me sleep?" Wesley yelled.

"You get up right this moment young man, we have lots of things to do."

"Oh, right this is going to be a great day, carry burlap bags, ice cream freezers, and dress up in that monkey suit for the wedding and carry that silly ring on that girly pillow. This day and night is going to go on and on."

He continued. .

"Wes, you stop your moaning, we all have things to do." Phil said walking down the hallway to the stairs.

"Let's get going we will have a good day if we all work together." "I'm tired and I want to sleep some more." Wes sighed.

"Up and at it now I said." Phil said smacking Wes on the bottom.

"Oh, that hurts, now I'm getting beaten by my own father."

"You will get more if you don't get up this minute." Phil said.

"All right, all right, I'm getting up, leave me alone and I'll get ready."

Phil slipped up behind Irene and grabbed her around the waist causing her to throw a scone on the floor.

"Oh, Phil, I didn't hear you."

"Sorry, just wanted a hug." He said giving her a kiss and a hug.

"You two stop it, you are always doing that." Marilee said.

Phil asked.

"It looks silly; you both look too old to be doing that sort of thing." She replied.

"Too old?" Irene asked.

"Too old, and silly you shouldn't be doing that. Act like grownups should. My friend's parents don't do that."

"I am sure they do, you just haven't seen them and we don't care you can look the other way, I am not going to stop hugging your mother." Phil winked at Irene.

"Let's eat, Wes did you wash your hands?"

"Yes mum I did."

"Go get the boys to come in for breakfast, please?" Irene smiled.

"Oh all right I will." Wes said running out to the boy's cottage.

***

"Olive, where is my suit for tonight?" Ron asked.

"Look in the drying cupboard, it should be there."

"Yes, I see it, good, wanted to be sure everything was in order when we come back to get ready for the wedding and the celebration."

"Good, glad you found it. Help me put the baskets in order.

Is Nigel up?" Olive asked.

"Yes, he's moving boxes for me and line them up for loading to take to the commons."

"Wonderful, how is his eye?"

"Black and puffy, but not bad for the fight he had last night at the pub. He doesn't remember what it was all about.

Maybe he can find out today. I don't think he is ever going to stop drinking do you?" Ron asked.

"No, I sure hate to watch him go through life going from one problem to another caused from drinking too much."

"Me too, it is such a waste."

***

Cinny ran around the cottage in daze thinking about everything at once and how the wedding would go and the celebration she and Annie still had to prepare food and organize their helpers to do the things they had planned.

"Cinny, slow down you will work yourself into a state and be worn out by six o'clock. What can I do to help you calm down?' Annie asked.

"I don't know, there is so much to think about getting ready I wanted to make sure everything was on track." She sighed sitting down for a cup of tea.

"Everything will be fine we have gone over and over everything them and they know what to do and when. All you need to do is be as beautiful as you can for your wedding. Take a long hot bath later and do your hair and Rita will comb it for you. She said she would put you on her schedule at the beauty shop but will come here to comb it for you. We are all organized my little sister. I am going to miss you so much. Thank goodness for Uncle Reggie and Auntie Lily."

CHAPTER FORTY THREE

The wedding music filled the old church and brought a welcomed feeling to know one of their favorite couples in the village would be the first to get married since the war ended.

Many wondered how many more weddings would be coming in the future.

Collin stood stiff and wiped sweat from his brow and forehead as he finished dressing for the wedding.

"Matt, you look great in that black tux; Les did a great job on all of ours didn't he?"

"He did, I was surprised the fitting went so smoothly for us all. Since he stopped drinking his work is much improved."

"I was thinking the same thing. Wish Nigel would quit, maybe later. I can't believe how nervous I am. I didn't think once that would happen since I was so happy to begin my new life with Cinny in Oxford and never thought about 'wedding jitters.'"

"Sorry, about that but I'll be right beside you and it won't be long and your new life will begin. You and Cinny will be happy forever."

"There is the song signal for us to take our place at the front of the Chapel. Let's go."

The two friends stood silently in front of the vicar turning to watch for the wedding procession to begin.

Marilee started her walk down the long aisle of the church throwing a few pink petals at a time. Her long hair piled up on her head made her feel grown up. She found herself enjoying her part of the wedding. She was happy with the pretty pink and white floral dress Irene had made for her. She felt grown up.

Wesley followed holding the pink satin pillow straight out in front of him felling like his arms were wooden boards.

Annie held the arm of Collin's friend from the war as they walked to the front where the two friends and the vicar was waiting for them. The two other couples of bridesmaids and grooms men followed them.

Cinny and Uncle Reggie waited for a few seconds to start the bridal song and everyone stood up when it began.

She felt like she was in a dream and hoped she wouldn't wake up and hoped that this was the real thing the start of her new life with the man she loved.

Her feelings of loss at not being able to see Annie everyday was still a sad part of their new adventure in Oxford.

Her long white train was carried by two of the children related to Polly.

"Collin, Cinny is outstandingly beautiful in that gown. She looks more grown up into a stunning woman. You are lucky my lad." Matt whispered to the shaking Collin.

"I know, she is stunning." He whispered back, his heart pounding even more than before.

When Cinny stood beside Collin she felt her hands shake and instantly could feel her bridegroom shaking as well.

The vicar sensed the nervous couple and whispered to them he hadn't lost a couple yet and they could relax and smile.

They each took a deep breath and the nuptials began.

Annie glanced over at Matt noticing how handsome he looked in the tux. She felt for the first time he wasn't that pesky little boy that had spent his life annoying her.

He caught her glance and winked at her making her realize the feelings that were stirring inside at that moment. She looked away not wanting to accept the reaction to his wink.

Collin and Cinny said the last of their vows and the vicar said the words, "You may now kiss the bride."

With that Collin swept her up into his arms reaching for the veil and placed it back from her face.

They ran down the aisle as the family and friends made their way to the commons for the reception and celebration which they had set up before the wedding so all they had to do was celebrate both occasions.

The commons had the aura of one ending and a new beginning for them all. The war had brought them all close together as a large family. They had helped each other through many sad and frightening days and nights.

Dressed in their best clothes the villagers took their places at the tables they had earlier set up for the reception.

The sun was going down and turned the sky from a golden glow slowly into the purple hue of early evening.

The Paper Yellow Moon Matt had Reggie make over the cardboard sea hung in the air with the backdrop of the darkening English Channel was even more beautiful than Matt had hoped. Everything came together so smoothly he couldn't help but feel maybe this would be the night that Annie might let him know about their future and if they had one.

His father and Collin's had made it to the wedding and was happy everything was turning out so well for all of them.

Not feeling guilty about dumping their businesses on their sons they both raised a glass to each other for their new futures away from Brooker's Village.

The band began to play the favorite Glen Miller music and Collin brought Cinny to the dance floor for the first dance.

Matt looked at Annie and walked over to her and took her by the arm to the floor. She followed with a thumping heart and shaky hands followed him.

"Well, Miss Brooker, I would imagine you will be getting married someday."

"I suppose so, is this proposal?"

"Let me think, well, I suppose it is." He laughed as he danced her over under the paper moon.

"You suppose so?"

"Now my love, don't get snitty with me I have the ring and am ready when you are, I have just been waiting for me to grow up and you find a sense of humor."

"That's a nice thing to say, what kind of proposal is that?"

"It is the best one I can think of at the moment, are you ready to marry a younger man?"

"If you promise never to tease me about being older I will say yes. You must promise though."

"I promise I will never call you an older woman." He laughed.

"You don't sound serious and I am very serious about that label, older woman."

"What can I say to make you believe me, that I will never call you an older woman?"

"I guess I shall have to trust you, won't I?"

"Yes, my darling you will have to trust me. I promise I shall never hurt you Miss Brooker and we will have a wonderful future together."

Matt said as he stopped under the yellow moon and kissed her as he had dreamed about for so long, yes, he finally had the reassuring feeling that they would have a happy future in Brooker's Village-On Sea.

THE END

www.ingramcontent.com/pod-product-compliance
Lightning Source LLC
Chambersburg PA
CBHW021709120626
46545CB00004B/1480